The Treasury of Clean Jokes

Tal D. Bonham

BROADMAN PRESS
Nashville, Tennessee

To the memory of Elgene Phillips
who enjoyed good humor on earth
and now rejoices in heaven
and
To my four funny kids: Marilyn,
Randy, Daniel, and Tal David

4257-03
ISBN: 0-8054-5703-8
Dewey Decimal Classification: 808.7
Subject heading: JOKES
Library of Congress Catalog Card Number: 80-67639

Printed in the United States of America

Foreword

The Value of a Smile

It costs nothing, but creates much good. It enriches those who receive it without impoverishing those who give it away. It happens in a flash but the memory of it can last forever. No one is so rich that he can get along without it. No one is too poor to feel rich when receiving it. It creates happiness in the home, fosters goodwill in business, and is the countersign of friends. It is rest to the weary, daylight to the discouraged, sunshine to the sad, and nature's best antidote for trouble.

Yet it cannot be bought, begged, borrowed, or stolen for it is something of no earthly good to anybody until it is given away willingly.

ANONYMOUS

Acknowledgments

How do you document jokes? Frankly, it is impossible. Many of the jokes in this book were heard at civic clubs and church gatherings. Some were caught in conversation or from radio or television. For years, I have clipped and recorded jokes and filed them for future use. When the opportunity to compile this book presented itself, I sat down and recalled many of the "oldies but goodies" which were not on file.

I am indebted to Mrs. Opal Koonce, my secretary, for her help and encouragement in this venture. My wife, Faye, was so patient to help in the "culling process" by listening to most of these jokes read aloud. All four of my children helped at some time or another throughout the whole process.

Introduction

Comedian Jerry Lewis calls humor a "safety valve." "The peoples of the world who have the ability to laugh at themselves are those who survive," he claims.

Bob Hope says that laughter has constructive power. A laugh, he says, "can transform almost unbearable tears into something bearable, even hopeful."

Country humorist Jerry Clower says, "God doesn't want his children to walk around unhappy. He wants them to be happy. I am convinced that there is just one place where there is just not any laughter and that is hell. And I've made arrangements to miss hell, so, ha, ha, ha, I ain't goin' to have to ever be nowhere some folks ain't laughin'."

An after-dinner speaker fed his audience a sordid diet of obscene stories punctuated with profanity. Midway in his presentation, he noticed that one of the guests at the head table wasn't laughing. He stopped, looked at him, and noticed a chaplain's insignia in the lapel of his suit. Embarrassed, the speaker blurted out, "For Christ's sake, are you a chaplain?"

"Yes, for Christ's sake I am a chaplain, for whose sake are you telling these filthy stories?" asked the chaplain. There was an outburst of laughter, applause, and then silence. The chaplain was then asked to speak, at which time he stood and gave a clean, cheerful speech.

Who said that good humor can't be clean? In fact, the Bible has a great deal to say about a sense of humor. Centuries ago Solomon said, "A merry heart doeth good like a medicine: but a broken spirit drieth the bones" (Prov. 17:22). Just listen to these words from the Bible concerning humor:

A merry heart maketh a cheerful countenance; but by sorrow of the heart the spirit is broken (Prov. 15:13).

He that is of a merry heart hath a continual feast (Prov. 15:15).

Be glad in the Lord, and rejoice, ye righteous; and shout for joy, all ye that are upright in heart (Ps. 32:11).

Jesus said, "Be of good cheer, I have overcome the world" (John 16:33). After his death, burial, and resurrection, his disciples were scattered all over the world, proclaiming the good news of the gospel. A typical reaction to the gospel was found in Samaria: "There was great joy in that city" (Acts 8:8). One of the watchwords of the apostle Paul was, "Rejoice in the Lord alway: and again I say, Rejoice" (Phil. 4:4).

Because Christians have found the secret of real happiness, they, of all people, can and should enjoy clean humor. It is with this conviction that this book was written. I hope you enjoy it and will find some humorous material you can pass on to others.

Contents

Absentmindedness

An absentminded professor fell down a flight of stairs. He struggled to his feet, picked up his glasses from the floor and put them on. Brushing off his clothes, he looked up the stairs and remarked, "I wonder who made all that noise?"

Caller: "Is this 789-4383?"
Professor: "No, this is 789-4384."
Caller: "Oh, I have the wrong number. I'm sorry to have bothered you."
Professor: "That's quite all right. I had to get up to answer this phone anyway."

One of the world's greatest scientists was also recognized as the original absentminded professor. One day on board a train, he was unable to find his ticket. The conductor said, "Take it easy. You'll find it."

When the conductor returned, the professor still couldn't find the ticket. The conductor, recognizing the famous scientist, said, "I'm sure you bought a ticket. Forget about it."

"You're very kind," he said, "but I must find it, otherwise I won't know where to get off."

A husband-and-wife vaudeville team returned to their dressing room at the Palladium in London to find a thief had taken their jewelry.

They called Scotland Yard and a detective arrived, complete with derby, pipe, and umbrella. He questioned everyone so thoroughly that there was no doubt in anyone's mind but that the jewels would be recovered.

The following day there was a phone call. "This is Inspector Gray of Scotland Yard."

"Yes, yes," answered the comedian. "You've found our jewels?"

"No, but have you found my umbrella? I think I left it in your dressing room."

"Doctor, I have this terrible problem; I can't remember a thing," exclaimed an anxious lady to her doctor.

"How long have you had this problem?" the doctor asked.

"What problem?" she replied.

Aging

The five *B*'s of old age: baldness, bursitis, bifocals, bulges, and bunions.

An elderly farm couple saw a motorcycle coming down the road. Not knowing what it was, they became frightened. The woman ran and hid under the bed. The man ran behind the door and peeked through the crack.

He said to his wife, "That thing's comin' and its got a man."

He reached for his shotgun, took aim, and shot.

"Did you get it?" his wife asked.

"I don't know," he replied, "but I sure made it let go of that man."

OLD AGE: When the gleam in your eye is just the sun on your bifocals.

The quack was selling a potion which he declared would make one live to a ripe old age.

"Look at me," he shouted, "hale and hearty. I'm over three hundred years old."

"Is he really as old as that?" asked a listener of the young assistant.

"I can't say," replied the assistant, "I've only worked for him a hundred years."

Man: "How old are you, my little man?"

Child: "Darned if I know, Mister. Mother was twenty-six when I was born and now she's only twenty-four."

Just when you're successful enough to sleep late, you're so old you always wake up early.

Frequent naps prevent old age, especially if taken while driving.

The train was bound for Miami. The conductor was collecting tickets. He spied a figure crouched beneath a seat. He approached and saw it was a little, old, wrinkled man. "Let's have your ticket," he demanded.

The old man crawled out of his hiding place. "Please Sir," he begged, "I don't have a ticket. I'm poor. I can't afford one. But my only daughter is getting married in Miami tonight. I've got to get there for the wedding."

A gentle and sentimental man, the conductor was visibly touched by the story.

"OK," he muttered. "You can ride the train. But sit in the men's room and keep out of the way."

The conductor then continued down the aisle. He spied another old man hiding behind a seat. "You there," he shouted, "where's your ticket?"

Said the oldster, "What ticket? I don't know anything about a ticket. My friend invited me to the wedding."

At a dinner party several of the guests were arguing whether men or women were more trustworthy. "No woman," said one man scornfully, "can keep a secret."

"I don't know about that," huffily answered a woman guest. "I have kept my age a secret since I was twenty-one."

"You'll let it out some day," the man insisted.

"I hardly think so," responded the lady. "When a woman has kept a secret for twenty-seven years, she can keep it forever."

Husband to a friend: "It's terrible to grow old alone. My wife hasn't had a birthday in ten years!"

Several elderly church members were being asked the secret of their longevity.

"And why do you think God has permitted you to reach the age of ninety-two?" one sweet lady was asked.

Without hesitation she responded, "To test the patience of my relatives."

One man found the key to safe driving for his wife. He reminded her that if she had an accident, the newspapers would print her age with the police report.

Three retirees, each with a hearing loss, were taking a walk one fine March day. One remarked to the other, "Windy, ain't it?"

"No," the second man replied, "It's Thursday."

And the third man chimed in, "So am I, let's have a Coke."

According to statistics, by the time a man reaches the age of seventy, there are five women for every man. What a time for the odds to change.

It Got-up and Went

How do I know my youth is all spent?
My get-up-and-go has got up and went.
My joints are still and filled with pain.
The pills that I take they give me no gain.
I rub in the ointment like fury I do,
Each pain when it leaves, comes back with two.

But in spite of it all I am able to grin
When I think of the places my get-up has been.

Old age is GOLDEN I have heard it said,
But sometimes I wonder as I get into bed—
My "ears" on the dresser, my "teeth" in a cup,
My "eyes" on the table until I wake up.
Ere sleep comes each night I say to myself,
"Is there anything else I should lay on the shelf?"
Yet I am happy to know as I close the door.
My friends are the same as in days of yore.

. . . .

Since I have retired from life's competition
Each day is filled with complete repetition.
I get up every morning and dust off my wits
Go pick up the paper and read the "o-bits."
If my name isn't there I know I'm not dead;
I get a good breakfast and go back to bed.
The reason I know my youth is all spent—
My get-up-and-go has got-up and went.

AUTHOR UNKNOWN

Bob Hope once said, "Today my heart beat 103,369 times, my blood traveled 168 million miles, I breathed 23,400 times, I inhaled 438 cubic feet of air, I ate 3 pounds of food, drank 2.9 pounds of liquid, I perspired 1.43 pints, I gave off 85.3 degrees of heat, I generated 450 tons of energy, I spoke 4,800 words, I moved 750 major muscles, my nails grew .00056 inches, my hair grew .01714 inches, and I exercised 7 million brain cells. Gee, but I'm tired."

Little Janie was sitting on her grandfather's knee one day and after looking at him intently for some time, she said, "Grandpa, were you in the ark with Noah?"

"Certainly not, my dear," he replied in astonishment.

"Then," asked the child, "why weren't you drowned?"

When a sudden storm blew up at sea, a young woman, leaning against the ship's rail, lost her balance and was thrown overboard. Immediately another figure plunged into the waves beside her and held her up until a lifeboat rescued them. To everyone's astonishment the hero was the oldest man on the voyage—an octogenarian. That evening he was given a party in honor of his bravery. "Speech! Speech!" the other passengers cried.

The old gentleman rose slowly and looked around at the enthusiastic gathering. "There's just one thing I'd like to know," he said testily. "Who pushed me?"

Airplanes

Customer: "I want a ticket to New York."

Airline Clerk: "By Buffalo?"

Customer: "I guess that's OK, if the saddle's comfortable."

Before the plane took off, the flight attendant gave chewing gum to all the passengers. "This will keep your ears from popping when we attain a high altitude," she told them.

After the plane had landed, a worried-looking man came over to the flight attendant. "This was my first flight," he told her. "It was very nice, but now that it's over, could you tell me how to get this gum out of my ears?"

An elderly woman, flying for the first time, was most happy to see the pilot as he walked down the aisle greeting passengers and inspecting the aircraft.

"Sir," said the little old lady, "you'll bring me down safely, won't you?"

"Of course," the captain answered. "I've never left anyone up here yet."

A pilot always looked down intently on a certain valley in the Appalachians. "What's so interesting about that spot?" asked a fellow pilot.

"See that stream? Well, when I was a kid, I used to sit down there on a log, fishing. Every time an airplane flew over, I would look up and wish I were flying. Now I look down and wish I were fishing."

Lady to flight attendant: "Tell the pilot not to fly faster than sound. My friend and I want to talk."

When his engine conked out, the pilot of a light plane glided to a landing on the New York State Thruway. The pilot jumped out and walked back to the only car in sight, which had pulled off the road out of his way, to ask for a lift to the closest interchange. As he neared the car, the woman sitting beside the driver stuck her head out the window and said excitedly, "We'll get out of the way, Mister, if you'll just show us where to go. This clown here is the only driver in the country who could start out on the Thruway and wind up in the middle of an airport!"

At a travel bureau a clerk was trying to convince a woman of the safety of air travel. She remained unconvinced until he threw in this clincher, "Madam, if it weren't safe, would we be using the 'fly now, pay later' plan?"

One morning a man called a taxi company and complained that a cab he ordered to take him to the airport had not arrived. The girl who took the call apologized, "I'm very sorry the cab isn't there yet, Sir," she said. "But don't worry, the plane is always late."

"Well, it certainly will be this morning." The caller said sharply, "I happen to be the pilot."

Here are some recently recorded announcements of various airline flight attendants.

In Germany: "Good evening. Welcome to the world's most superior airline. Please march to your seats, sit without squirming, ring for your hostess only when absolutely necessary."

In Israel: "We shall be flying at an altitude . . . you wouldn't believe it! Under your seat is a life jacket. You should wear it only in good health."

In Madrid: "Have a most pleasant flight, and please pray for clear skies because the planes in Spain fall mainly in the rains."

Riding in a propeller plane, the passengers saw three of the four engines conk out. The cabin door opened and the pilot appeared with a parachute on his back.

"Keep calm, folks, and don't panic—I'm going for help!"

Animals

The door swung open. A cowboy rushed out, took a running jump, and landed in the gutter.

"What's the matter with you, Fella?" asked a bystander. "Did they kick you out, or are you just plain loco?"

"Neither," said the cowboy, "but I sure would like to lay my hands on the person who moved my horse!"

A confused man was walking down a lonely country road one day, dragging a long rope behind him.

Upon being greeted by a friend coming down the road, he said, "I am so confused that I don't know whether I've found a rope or lost a mule."

A carrier pigeon showed up eleven hours late with his message.

When they asked him what happened, he said, "Nothing! It was just such a nice day I decided to walk!"

Did you hear about the pigeon who was walking around people-toed?

"Has your dog a good pedigree?"

"Has he? Say, if that dog could talk, he wouldn't speak to either of us!"

A Russian wolfhound and a French poodle met on a Paris street.

"How are things in Russia?" the poodle asked.

"Couldn't be better," the Russian wolfhound said. "I sleep in a solid gold doghouse on a carpet, and all day long they feed me caviar."

"If things are that great, why do you come to Paris?"

The Russian wolfhound looked around and whispered into the poodle's ear, "Sometimes I like to bark!"

"Glad to see you are getting to school on time these mornings," said the teacher.

"Yes, Sir, I've got a parrot now."

"A parrot! Young man, I told you to get an alarm clock!"

"I never seem to hear alarm clocks," explained the student. "But, now I've got this parrot. And what the parrot says when the alarm wakes him up is enough to wake up anybody."

A customer walked into a pet shop and spied a parrot. He ambled over to the bird and said, "Hey, can you speak, Stupid?"

The bird answered, "Yes. Can you fly, Dummy?"

A friend of mine walked into a bar holding a duck in his arms. The bartender said to him, "Hey, Buddy, what you doing with that pig?"

My friend answered indignantly, "You must be blind. Can't you see this is a duck, not a pig?"

"I wasn't talking to you," said the bartender. "I was talking to the duck."

The young man had asked for a job with the circus—any job just so he could travel with the circus.

The owner of the circus, thinking he might be able to make an assistant lion tamer out of the young man, took him out to the practice cage.

The head lion tamer, a beautiful young woman, was just starting her rehearsal. As she entered the cage, she removed her cape with a flourish and, standing in a gorgeous costume, motioned to one of the lions.

Obediently the lion crept toward the young woman, licked her elbow, and rolled over twice.

"Well," said the owner to the young man, "think you could do that?"

"I'm sure I could, Sir," said the young man, "but first you'll have to get that lion out of there."

Two monkeys were in a space capsule on their way to the moon. One complained about the situation. The other said, "This is better than working in the cancer clinic."

"Just think," said the man reading his magazine, "It says here that over 5,000 camels are used each year to make paint brushes!"

"Goodness," answered the woman, impressed. "Isn't it amazing what they can teach animals these days?"

The sheriff of a small mountain town was also the veterinarian. Late one night the phone rang. An excited voice asked, "Is Lem there?"

"Yes," his wife replied. "Do you want him in his capacity as vet or sheriff?"

"Both," came the reply. "We can't get our new bulldog to open his mouth and there's a burglar in it."

Picnicker: "Is this bull safe?"
Farmer: "He's a lot safer than you are right now."

The maid had just been discharged. Extracting five dollars from her purse, she threw it to Fido, the family dog.

When asked why by her former employer, she answered, "I never forget a friend. This was for helping me clean the dishes all this time."

A little boy who had spent a week at a dude ranch told his mother excitedly: "Mom, I even saw a man who makes horses."

"Are you sure?" asked his mother.

"Yes," he replied. "He had a horse nearly finished when I saw him, and he was just nailing on the feet."

Teacher (pointing to a deer at the zoo): "Curtis, what is that?"
Curtis: "I don't know."
Teacher: "What does your mother call your father?"
Curtis: "Don't tell me that's a louse!"

The lady visiting a mink farm wished to display her profound interest in the fur business. She asked brightly, "And how many mink skins do you get from each animal?"

"Only one, lady," replied the owner. "If we try to skin them twice it makes them nervous."

"Clara," said the mistress to the new maid, "you may now take the dog and give him some air."

"Yes, Ma'am. Where is the nearest filling station?"

A press agent arranged for an audition with a well-known TV producer for his client, a talking dog. The skeptical producer warmed up as the dog started with a joke or two, then went into an amusing political satire. The press agent pointed out that his client really wanted to be a singer. After several songs, the producer was convinced that this was a gold mine. Just then, a huge, ugly dog burst into the audition room, grabbed the little dog by the neck, and bounded out of the room. The producer wildly turned to the press agent, who was slowly putting on his coat, for an explanation.

"That's his mother," he said dejectedly. "She wants him to be a doctor."

A man who was walking his dog one afternoon ran into a little girl walking her poodle.

"What a beautiful puppy," he said. "Do you have papers with it?"

"We sure do," the girl replied, "all over the floor."

Fleas must face the tragic fact that their children usually go to the dogs.

An agent with a shaggy, mongrel dog called on the producer of a TV variety show. "Max," said the agent, "you can have this mutt for twenty bucks."

"Why should I buy that mutt for twenty bucks?"

"Because he's a talking dog."

"Listen," said the producer, "I'm sick and tired of that talking dog routine. I've got no time to kid around. Take the mutt and get lost."

Suddenly the dog jumped up on the producer's desk.

"Please, Sir," he began, "have the goodness of heart to purchase me from this brute. I know I don't look like the most attractive dog in the world. But that's not entirely my fault. My present master never feeds me. Once in a while he throws me a scrap. He's an agent. Let's face it, Mr. Producer! Do you know anyone as low, miserable, dishonest, conniving, cheap, and unprincipled as an agent?

"This man," the dog continued, "has made a fortune booking me into the largest theaters and night clubs all over the world. I have played for presidents, noblemen, dignitaries, the crowned heads of Europe, the sheiks of Arabia. I plead with you, Sir. Buy me from this rascal, and I will make you half a million the first year."

The producer was amazed at the dog's fluency, his power of speech, the extent of his vocabulary. "For Pete's sake," he finally managed, "this dog talks like a Rhodes scholar. Why do you want to sell him to me for twenty bucks?"

"Because," said the agent, "I'm fed up to the ears with his constant lying."

There was a mouse who committed suicide when he found out his father was a rat.

Automobiles

Thought: There's a line on the ocean where you lose a day when you cross it.

Afterthought: There's a line on the highway where you can do even better.

An Englishman, an Irishman, and an American were flying over the Sahara Desert.

The Englishman observed, "A beastly place."

The Irishman exclaimed, "The devil's home."

The American exulted, "What a parking lot!"

A man stood on a street corner waiting in vain for the heavy traffic to thin out so he could cross. Finally, as he was about to take his chances, he spied a man on the other side and called to him, "Say, how did you get over there?"

The other man cupped his hands about his mouth. "Easy," he shouted, "I was born over here!"

Interstates are so efficient and well-engineered that you can get on a throughway and be in a large city in a neighboring state in just five hours — *whether you want to or not.*

Filling station attendant: "Your oil is OK, but your engine needs changing."

Driver: "I had to drive into a fence to keep from hitting a cow down the road."
Farmer: "Was it a Jersey cow?"
Driver: "I don't know — I didn't check her license plate."

Mechanic to owner of old broken-down car: "Let me put it this way — if your car were a horse, it would have to be shot."

Most cities have only two types of pedestrians — the quick and the dead.

While driving along a main street in a busy city, a lady was stopped by a policeman who was spot-checking cars. After testing the brakes, lights, and horn, the officer asked to see her driver's license.

"It says here 'corrective lenses.' Why aren't you wearing glasses?" he demanded.

"I've got contacts," replied the lady.

The officer exploded! "I don't care who you know. You're supposed to be wearing glasses!"

As the motorist put it when he wrapped his new sports car around a telephone pole: "Well, that's the way the Mercedes Benz!"

A man who wasn't accustomed to city traffic and city parking lots lamented to a passerby that he couldn't remember where he had parked his car.

"Why don't you take the bus?"

"Shucks, friend, they ain't no use in takin' a bus, it wouldn't fit in my garage."

After knocking down a woman pedestrian who was jay-walking, the cab driver stopped and helped the irate lady to her feet.

Refusing his assistance, she shrieked, "You stupid, reckless creature! You must be blind!"

"What do you mean, blind?" snapped the hackie. "I hit you, didn't I?"

"Car sickness is that feeling you get every month when the payment falls due."

Drive carefully. Remember a car is not the only thing that can be recalled by its maker.

"Have you ever driven a car?" the lady applicant for a license was asked.

"One hundred and twenty thousand miles," put in her husband, "and she's never had a hand on the wheel!"

A man returned to his parked automobile, found the front crumpled, but the car that hit him had gone.

His spirits brightened momentarily when he saw a note under his windshield wiper. It read: "There are at least twenty people watching while I write this. They think I am putting down my name, address, and phone number. But I'm not!"

One cold night a man with reputedly poor eyesight was driving a friend home. The frost was thick on the windows. After a couple of near accidents, the friend tactfully suggested that it might help if they cleaned off the windshield.

"What's the use?" the driver replied. "I left my glasses at home."

Banking

The modern American is a person who drives a bank-financed car over a bond-financed highway on a credit card.

A man in Wichita, Kansas, received a computerized bill for nothing. The balance due column read $00.00. He threw it away.

A month later the same store sent another bill with the following notation: "This account is now past due."

He circled the zeros and sent the bill back to the store.

A few days later he received another scorching computerized letter. It admonished him to pay his debt of $00.00. Realizing that nothing can be quite as stubborn as a computer, he finally sat down and wrote out a check for $00.00. He received no further pleas from the store.

Said the FBI agent to the bank teller after the bank was robbed for the third time by the same thief, "Did you notice anything special about the robber?"

"Yes, he seemed to be better dressed each time."

"What is your name, Sir?" the bank teller asked politely.

"Don't you see my signature?" snapped the indignant patron.

"Yes, Sir. That's what aroused my curiosity."

One day a farmer came into the bank in Oklahoma and asked for a loan. "I want $200."

"And what security have you?"

"I have 200 horses," replied the farmer.

This seemed sufficient security and the loan was made. A short while afterward the farmer came back with $2,200 in cash, paid off the note and started to leave with the rest of the roll in his pocket.

"Why not let me take care of that money for you?" asked the banker.

Looking the banker straight in the eye, the farmer asked, "How many horses do *you* have?"

A wealthy Texas oilman cashed a huge personal check which came back from the bank with "Insufficient Funds" stamped across the face.

Beneath the stamped words was the handwritten notation: "Not you, us."

Bible

Auctioneer: "What am I offered for this beautiful bust of Robert Burns?"

Man in Crowd: "That's not Burns, it's Shakespeare."

Auctioneer: "Well, folks, that's one on me. Shows how little I know about the Bible."

A keen lover of rare books met an unbookish guy who had just thrown away an old Bible (packed away for generations in the attic of his ancestral home).

"Somebody named Guten-something had printed it," he added.

"Not Gutenberg!" gasped the book lover. "You've thrown away one of the very first books ever printed. One copy sold at auction recently for over $400,000."

The other man, still unmoved, said, "Oh, my copy wouldn't have brought a dime—some fellow named Martin Luther had scribbled notes all over it."

Danny: "Why does your grandmother read the Bible so much?"

David: "I think she's cramming for her finals."

Helping his wife wash the dishes, a minister protested, "This isn't a man's job."

"Oh, yes, it is," his wife retorted, quoting 2 Kings 21:13: "I will wipe Jerusalem as a man wipeth a dish, wiping it, and turning it upside down."

An eight-year-old boy had been pestering his father for a watch. Finally his father said in exasperation, "I don't want to hear about your wanting a watch again."

At dinner that night the family each gave a Scripture verse at the dinner table, and the boy repeated Mark 13:37. "And what I say unto you I say unto all, Watch."

Business

At an annual hotel owners' convention a roving commentator, mike in hand, approached a world-famous hotel man. Holding up the mike, he said, "Sir, your name has become synonymous with the hotel business. You have expanded your chain to all corners of the globe, offering the peoples of the world a comfortable home away from home. Do you have a word, Sir? All America is listening and watching!"

"Yes, thank you," said the hotel magnate, "I do have a word for all America. Please keep the shower curtains on the inside!"

Applicants for jobs on a dam project in Nevada had to take a written examination. The first question was, "What does hydrodynamics mean?" One guy hesitated, then wrote, "It means I don't get the job."

Well! They finally did it. They're constructing a $10 million hotel right in the heart of Moscow. It will be called the "Comrade Hilton."

My favorites, of all the days,
Are Saturday and Sunday
If only these delightful days
Weren't followed then by Monday.

A fellow on a film crew spent several months in the Congo filming. He collected a trunkful of shrunken heads. He decided they might be worth something. So, when he returned to Hollywood, he called up Saks Fifth Avenue, Beverly Hills.

"To whom do I speak about selling some shrunken heads?" he asked the switchboard operator.

She told him to wait a moment. Then there was a clicking sound and a firm, businesslike voice said, "This is the head buyer speaking."

Curt: "They tell me you're the man who invented spaghetti. Where did you ever get the idea for it?"
Randy: "Out of my noodle."

A businessman had two windows in his office. One was easy to raise and the other always gave him trouble — so he labeled one "his" and the other "hernia."

"It's not just the work I enjoy," said the taxi driver. "It's the people I run into."

Keep your eye on the ball, your shoulder to the wheel, your ear to the ground, and your nose to the grindstone. Now try to work in that position.

Bystander: "I see you are putting up a new building."

Foreman: "This company has a strict policy. We never put up an old one."

"I've worked here for eight years," an overworked employee said to her boss, "and I've been doing the work of three people. I want a raise."

"I can't give you a raise," the boss answered. "But if you'll tell me who the other two people are I'll fire them."

"Why did you leave your last job?" asked the manager.

"Illness," said the job applicant.

"What kind of illness?"

"I don't know," the man said. "They just said they were sick of me."

After forty years of hard work, Smith retired with a comfortable fortune of $90,000 which he had gained through courage, diligence, initiative, skill, devotion to duty, thrift, efficiency, shrewd investment, and the death of an uncle who left him $89,999.50.

It's all right to begin at the bottom — except in learning to swim.

Note in the pay envelope: "Your raise will become effective as soon as you do."

A young businessman was running to catch the morning train from far out suburbia to the city. Trotting up to a farmer, he asked, "Say, do you mind if I take a shortcut across your field? I want to catch the 6:45."

"Sure, go ahead, young feller," replied the farmer, "but if my bull sees you, you'll catch the 6:15."

COMMITTEE MEETINGS: A person gets up and speaks and says nothing. Nobody listens, then everybody disagrees with him.

Boss: "This is the end. You're fired!"
Worker: "Fired? I thought slaves were sold!"

After examining the contents of the employees' suggestion box, the boss complained, "I wish they'd be more specific. What kind of kite? What lake?"

Advertisement for a handkerchief factory: "Let us stick your nose in our business."

Have you heard about the manicurist who married a pedicurist? They waited on each other hand and foot.

A retailer sent an order to a distributor for a sizable amount of goods. The distributor wired him, "Can't ship until you pay for your last consignment."

The retailer's answer (collect) was, "Can't wait that long. Cancel order."

The company president summoned the sales manager for a momentous conference. "George," he began, "when you went to work for us, you started at the bottom. Two years later you were traffic manager. Your progress was equally striking in production, and you were the youngest plant superintendent in our history. As head of the sales department, your record is no less distinguished.

"Now I must consider the company's future. Effective immediately, I am resigning to open the way for a younger man. I am happy to inform you that you are to succeed me as president."

The sales manager blushed and gulped, "Gee!" he exclaimed, "gee, thanks, Dad!"

A wealthy contractor liked to know all about the employees who toiled in his vast business. One day he came upon a new young man who was expertly counting out a large wad of the firm's cash into pay envelopes.

"Where did you get your financial training, young man?" he asked.

"Yale," replied the young man.

"Good, good!" exclaimed the contractor, being a staunch advocate of higher learning. "What's your name?"

"Yackson."

A man had posted himself in front of an office building with a tray of shoelaces. One executive made it a daily habit to give the unfortunate a quarter, but he never took the laces. One day the peddler, on receiving the quarter, tapped his departing benefactor on the back: "I don't like to complain, Sir, but the laces have now gone up to 35¢."

The big business executive was in the waiting room on the maternity floor of the hospital. While other expectant fathers paced the floor and thumbed nervously through magazines, he sat at a table working furiously at a sheaf of papers he had taken from his bulging brief case.

After some hours a nurse came into the room and spoke to him. "It's a boy, Sir," she said.

"Well," snapped the executive without looking up from his work, "ask him what he wants."

A butcher who had just one chicken went back into the back of the store to make it appear that he was picking out the best one from a coop full. He went back, slammed the coop, and cackled like a chicken and came back with the one and only chicken that he had to sell Mrs. Jones.

He weighed it and said, "Mrs. Jones, that comes to $1.98." Mrs. Jones said, "Well, if you don't mind I would like one just a little larger."

So he went back into the back of the store and made more noises, came back with the same chicken, and said it cost $2.25.

Mrs. Jones replied, "I believe I will take both of them."

A monastic order was low on funds and decided to set up a fish and chips stand outside the monastery, which bordered a busy street. The very first customer came up to the counter and with a smirk asked Brother Alfred, "Are you the fish friar?"

"No," said Brother Alfred with a straight face, "I'm the chip monk."

Children

After driving to a homestead to deliver the family's eleventh child, the physician said to the father when he opened the door, "I almost ran over a duck out there. Is it yours?"

"That's no duck," sighed the father. "It's the stork with its legs worn down."

David: "Today in school, a kid said I looked just like you."

Proud Pop: "And what did you say?"

David: "Nothing. He was a lot bigger than I am."

Two small boys at a modern art exhibit stared at a wildly abstract painting.

One of the youngsters muttered to the other, "Let's get out of here before they say we did it."

A nine-year-old wanted to impress his father. One evening, his father came along as he was playing with a bat and ball. "Watch me, Pop," he screamed. "I'm hitting them a mile."

He tossed the ball in the air, swung at it, and missed. "Strike one," he yelled gleefully.

Again he threw the ball in the air, swung, and missed again. "Strike two," he shouted. "Am I going to clout the next one!"

He took his stance carefully, tossed the ball in the air, and missed again.

"Strrrrrike three," he announced, "and out!" Then proudly, "Boy, oh, boy, am I a pitcher!"

Mother: "Do you think we should take Junior to the zoo?"

Father: "Absolutely not. If they want him, let them come for him."

The first thing a child learns when he gets a drum is that he's never going to get another one.

Father looking over his son's report card: "One thing is in your favor. With these grades you couldn't possibly be cheating."

Junior watched as dad finished a heavy meal and then loosened his belt.

"Look, Mom," he said, "Pop's just moved his decimal point over two places."

Eric didn't like soap and water. One day his mother was trying to reason with him. "Surely you want to be a clean little boy, don't you?"

"Yes," Eric agreed tearfully, "but can't you just dust me?"

Mother: "Did you thank Mrs. Jones for the lovely party she gave?"

Tommy: "No, Mommy. The girl leaving just before me thanked her and Mrs. Jones said, 'Don't mention it' — so I didn't."

"Children are a great comfort in your old age — and they help you reach it faster too."

A lady was entertaining the small son of a friend.

"Are you sure you can cut your own meat, Tommy?" she inquired.

"Oh, yes, thanks," answered the child politely. "I've often had it as tough as this at home."

Small boys are washable though most of them shrink from it.

The twelve-year-old's first letter home from summer camp read, "Send food. All they serve here is breakfast, lunch, and dinner."

A lady lost her handbag in the bustle of Christmas shopping. It was found by an honest little boy and returned to her.

Looking in her purse, she commented, "That's funny. When I lost my bag there was a $10 bill in it. Now there are ten $1 bills."

The boy quickly replied, "That's right, Lady. The last time I found a lady's purse, she didn't have any change for a reward."

Conversation heard at a boy's camp: "We're going home tomorrow. Guess I better rumple my pajamas and squeeze out half the toothpaste."

An exasperated mother to child at the dinner table: "Eat it, Dear. Pretend it's mud."

If you don't want your children to hear what you're saying, pretend you're talking to them.

"Is your mother home?" the salesman asked a small boy sitting on the steps in front of a house.

"Yeah, she's home," the boy said, scooting over to let him past.

The salesman rang the doorbell, got no response, knocked once, then again. Still no one came to the door.

Turning to the boy, the fellow said, "I thought you said your mother was home."

The kid replied, "She is; but this isn't where I live."

One of the mysteries of life is how the boy who wasn't good enough to marry your daughter can be the father of the smartest grandchild in the world.

Little Danny dashed into the drugstore. "Quick," he panted. "My father's hanging by his pants from the fence."

"What can I do?" asked the druggist.

"Put new film in my camera," said Danny.

Three Boy Scouts reported their good deed for the day, "We helped an old lady across the street."

"Did it take three to do that?"

"It sure did," they replied in unison. "She didn't want to go."

Two youngsters stood at the curb, waiting to cross the street, as the cars whizzed by in a frenzied fashion. Finally one turned to the other and asked: "What do you want to be if you grow up?"

A home with a four-year-old is a place where you also wash the soap when you clean the bathroom.

One blistering, hot day when guests were present for dinner, a mother asked her four-year-old son to say the blessing. "But, Mother, I don't know what to say," he protested.

"Just say what you've heard me say," she told him.

Obediently, he bowed his head and said, "Oh, Lord, why did I invite those people here on a hot day like this?"

Visitor: "Are your father and mother in?"
Child: "They was in but they is out."
Visitor: "Where's your grammar?"
Child: "She's upstairs."

Two Little Leaguers were taking a rest between innings. Suddenly, one of them spotted an extremely pretty little girl sitting in the front row of the bleachers. "Wow!" he exclaimed. "When I stop hating girls, she's the one I'd like to stop hating first."

A young mother who has four small children finds that her days are pretty hectic. Recently her husband, a systematic man, decided to help her make out a schedule.

On it they listed all of her chores and the exact time each one was to be done. The next evening he glanced at the schedule hanging in the kitchen. At the end of the list was this addition: "Call undertaker for free estimate."

"Danny," said Uncle Harley, "do you have a girl?

"Gosh, no," shouted the ten-year-old and ran off to his baseball game.

The little girl next door smiled wisely at Uncle Harley and said, "They're always the last ones to know."

A Western was showing at the neighborhood theater, and in one exciting scene the Indians had tied the heroine to a stake. They were setting fire to her and shooting arrows at her, when a voice in the theater was heard saying, "Dear, do you think I should call home and see how the sitter is getting along with the kids?"

Two small girls brought home a box full of dirt the other day and warned their mother to be very careful of it. "All right," she promised. "But tell me, why is it so special?"

"Instant mud pies," they answered.

A little boy said to his teacher, "I ain't got no pencil."

She corrected him at once: "It's 'I don't have a pencil.' 'You don't have a pencil.' 'We don't have any pencils.' 'They don't have any pencils.' Is that clear?"

"No," said the bewildered child. "What happened to all them pencils?"

A little girl had been particularly naughty all day and her exasperated mother finally sent her out in the backyard to get a switch off the peach tree. Considerable time elapsed, and the child didn't return. The mother called out the door for the child to come into the house at once, and "bring that switch with you." The youngster, her lips puckered and quivering, meekly appeared with her hands behind her back. "Well?" the mother said.

"I couldn't weach the peach tree," the child said, and then, holding out one hand, added, "but here's a wock you can frow at me."

Quiet reigned in the neighborhood when a family of ten went on vacation. A few days later the family next door received a postcard asking, "How are you enjoying our vacation?"

A little boy, taken to the ballet for the first time, watched curiously as the dancers cavorted about on their toes.

"Mom," he whispered loudly, "why don't they just get taller girls?"

A grade-school teacher was instructing her pupils in the value of coins. Taking out a half-dollar, she laid it on the desk and asked, "Can anyone tell me what that is?"

From the rear came the voice of a small boy, "Tails."

It was the first day of school and the kindergarten teacher asked the children what they wanted to be when they grew up. One little boy spoke up importantly:

"When I grow up, I'm gonna be a lion tamer. I'll have lots of fierce lions and tigers, and I'll walk in the cage . . ." he hesitated, then continued, "But, of course, I'll have my mother with me."

A beautiful little girl was playing in the park. An elderly man came by and remarked, "What a beautiful child you are. What is your name?"

The girl replied, "Shelley."

"Oh, what a lovely name," the man said. "How did your parents have the foresight to name you after a beautiful poet?"

The girl looked at him quizzically and answered, "Shelley Temple is a poet?"

An eight-year-old boy asked his father: "Dad, would you punish me for something I didn't do?"

"Of course not," said his father.

"Good," said the kid. "I didn't do my homework."

A five-year-old had one line in a kindergarten Christmas playlet, appearing in an angel's garb to say, "I bring you good tidings!"

After many rehearsals, the lad asked his mother what were "tidings." She explained tidings were news.

The performance began and the little angel became flustered. After a long embarrassing silence, he blurted out, "Hey, I got news for you!"

A little girl was showing her playmate through her new home.

"And here's my daddy's den," she said. "Does your daddy have a den?"

"No," was the answer, "my daddy just growls all over the house."

A Britisher was taken to a New York hotel. He and the room clerk became friendly and began swapping jokes.

The room clerk said to the Britisher, "I have a riddle: My mother and father had a baby. It wasn't my brother or my sister. Who was it?"

The visitor thought for a moment and said, "I don't know. Who was it?"

"It was me!" answered the clerk.

The Britisher, on his return to England, decided to try the riddle on his friend.

"My parents had a baby. It wasn't my brother or my sister. Who was it?"

His friend replied, "I don't know. Who was it?"

"The room clerk at a New York hotel," was the reply.

The little boy was scrutinizing his grandmother who had just arrived and whom he had never seen before.

"So you're my grandmother," he said.

"Yes," she replied sweetly, "on your father's side."

"Well, you're on the wrong side, I'll tell you that right now."

Two little boys came bursting into the house, shouting to their mother that the youngest brother had fallen into the lake.

"We tried giving him artificial respiration," one of them gulped, "but he kept getting up and running away."

A boy wrote to a pet dealer: "Sir, please send me two mongooses."

This didn't sound right, so he changed it to: "Sir, please send me two mongeese."

Still not satisfied he finally wrote, "Sir, please send me one mongoose. And while you're at it, send me another one."

Little Freddie was telling all, as he was discussing his new teacher. "She's mean, but she's fair," he said.

"How's that?" asked his mama.

"She's mean to everyone," he replied.

A young mother says that after putting her two children to bed one night she changed into a droopy blouse and an old pair of slacks and proceeded to wash her hair. While shampooing her hair, she could hear the children growing wilder and noisier. Finishing as hurriedly as possible, she wrapped a large towel around her head, stormed into their room and put them back to bed with a stern warning to stay there.

As she left, her two-year-old said in a trembling voice to his sister, "Who was that?"

A woman who runs a nursery school was delivering a station wagon load of kids home one day when a fire truck zoomed past. Sitting on the front seat was a Dalmatian. The children fell to discussing the dog's duties.

"They use him to keep the crowds back," said one five-year-old.

"No," said another, "he's just for good luck."

A third child brought the argument to an end. "They use the dog," he said firmly, "to find the fire plug!"

Church

The testimony meeting at church had gotten a little out of hand. One man stood and said, "I've been smoking three packages of cigarettes a day, and I'm going to quit."

"I've been drinking two cans of beer a day, and I'm going to quit," echoed another man.

"I've been cursing an awful lot, and I'm going to quit," confessed another parishioner.

Caught up in the excitement of the moment, a little old lady stood up and said, "I haven't been doing anything, and I'm going to quit."

If absence makes the heart grow fonder, think how much some people must love their church.

The pastor noticed a man who walked to the front of the auditorium for the service. Afterward the pastor spoke to the man and asked, "How was it that you came and sat right in front, being a stranger and all?"

"Oh," said the man, "I'm a bus driver, and I just came to see how you get everyone to sit in the rear of the building."

The census taker was asking all those questions—the ones that make sense and the ones that don't.

"And now," he said, "what's your church preference?"

Without batting an eye, the citizen replied, "Red brick."

An inactive church member had become critically ill with a heart attack. He inherited $10,000 from a deceased relative. His wife, thinking the shock of the good news might cause undue excitement, asked the pastor to break the news as gently as possible.

"Brother Jones," the pastor explained, "I know you have never tithed or given much to our church but God has been good to you anyway. He has given you a $10,000 inheritance."

"Great!" replied the fellow. "That means I can give a $1,000 tithe to the church next Sunday."

You guessed it! The pastor had a heart attack!

Most church members are 100 percent willing — 50 percent are willing workers and the other 50 percent are willing to let them.

A visiting evangelist was met at the end of the service with the blunt appraisal, "That's the worst sermon I have ever heard!"

The visiting preacher, quite disturbed, told the pastor that a certain man had said something rather critical and pointed him out.

The pastor said, "That man is not really responsible for what he says. He never has an original thought. He just goes around repeating what everybody else is saying."

These funny errors were picked out of orders of worship:

"O, Rest in the Lard"

"Blest Be the Tie That Blinds"

Sermon — "I'm Going to Kill Myself."

Invitation Hymn — "Why Do You Wait, Dear Brother?"

Sermon — "Between the Testaments: The Apocrypha"

Invitation Hymn — "Nothing Between"

Choral Worship — "When Jesus Speaks Your Name"

Sermon — "Are You Scared?"

Sermon — "The Most Hated King of Israel"

Invitation Hymn — "Only Trust Him"

Anthem — "In My Father's House Are Many Mansions."

Sermon — "Not Two, But One"

Anthem — "Jesus, Grant Me This I Pray"

Sermon — "Money! Money! Money!"

Sermon — "Samson's Head in the Lap of Delilah"

Invitation Hymn — "Leave It There"

Sermon — "Gossip"

Invitation Hymn — "I Love to Tell The Story"

The following announcements have been seen on church bulletin boards.

"No healing services Sunday due to the pastor's illness"

"Not everyone who enters this church has been converted, so please watch your handbags and wallets."

Sermon — "How Much Should a Christian Drink?"
Music By a Full Choir

"Come in and Get Your Faith Lifted."

Ladies, don't forget the rummage sale. It's a good chance to get rid of those things not worth keeping around the house. Bring your husbands.

The following announcements have been taken directly from church bulletins or weekly church papers.

Temperance Meeting: Members of the temperance

committee will meet in the home of Richard Smith, Thursday, February 10, 1979, at 7:30 PM—Drinks Will Be Furnished.

Clinic for Soul-Sinning Planned for January 5, 1979.

Mrs. Paul Berger will sink and Mrs. Wayne Webster will be at the organ. Mrs. Webster will play, "Throw Out The Lifeline."

Next Sunday: Mrs. G. C. is the soloist at the morning service. The pastor will speak on, "It's a Terrible Experience."

This afternoon there will be a meeting in the north and south ends of the church. Children will be baptized at both ends.

This being Easter Sunday, we will ask Mrs. B. to come forward and lay an egg on the altar.

When the collection plate was passed for the missionary offering, the little old lady began fumbling in her purse. The nearer the ushers came, the more frantically she searched her bag. Finally, noticing her plight, the little boy sitting nearby slid over and nudged her.

"Here lady," he said, "you take my dime; I can hide under the seat."

Anybody who thinks there's a shortage of coins hasn't been to church recently.

When it comes to giving, some people stop at nothing.

College

It was graduation day and Mom was trying to take a picture of their son in a cap and gown, posed with his father.

"Let's try to make this look natural," she said. "Junior, put your arm around your dad's shoulder."

The father answered, "If you want it to look natural, why not have him put his hand in my pocket?"

Rejected by the college of his choice, the banker's son angrily accosted his father. "If you really cared for me, you'd have pulled some wires!"

"I know," replied the parent sadly. "The TV, the stereo, and the telephone would have done for a start."

College professor to class: "If there are any dumbbells in this class, please stand up."

After a short pause, a strapping youth in the back of the room rose.

"So, you consider yourself a dumbbell?" the professor asked.

"No, Sir," replied the youth, "I just hated to see you standing there alone."

A Mother's Letter to Her Son in College

DEAR SON:

Just a few lines to let you know that I am still alive. I'm writing this letter slowly because I know that you cannot read very fast.

You won't know the house when you come home . . . we've moved.

About your father . . . he has a lovely job. He has 500 men under him. He is cutting the grass at the cemetery.

There was a washing machine in the new house when we moved in, but it isn't working too good. Last week I put fourteen shirts into it, pulled the chain, and I haven't seen the shirts since.

Your sister Mary had a baby this morning. I haven't found out whether it is a boy or girl, so I don't know whether you are an aunt or uncle.

Your Uncle Dick drowned last week in a vat of whiskey at the local brewery. Some of his work mates dived in to save him, but he fought them off bravely. We cremated his body and it took three days to put out the fire.

It rained only twice last week; first for three days, and then for four days. Monday it was so windy that one of the chickens laid the same egg four times.

We had a letter yesterday from the undertaker. He said if the last installment isn't paid on your grandmother within seven days, "up she comes."

Your Loving Mother

P.S. I was going to send you $50.00 but I had already sealed the envelope.

Ad in classified column of a university medical journal: "Will the person who stole the jar of alcohol from room 303 kindly return my uncle's appendix? No questions asked."

The mountain boy came home from college and his pa asked: "Whatcha learnin', Son?"

The boy said, "Well, Pa, I'm studying English."

"That's good, Son."

"And I'm studying algebra."

"That's fine, Son. Say something in algebra."

Not wanting to let the old man down, the boy thought a minute, then pronounced solemnly, "Pi-r-square."

The old man exploded, "If that's what they're learnin' ya, you kin stop school right now. Everyone knows pie are round and corn bread are square."

College is a place where nonconformists conform to the prevailing standard of nonconformity.

"What steps," a question in a college exam read, "would you take in determining the height of a building, using an aneroid barometer?"

One student, short on knowledge but long on ingenuity, replied, "I would lower the barometer on a string and measure the string."

A college education never hurt anyone who is willing to learn something afterward.

Student: "Were you out in all that rain, Professor?"

Professor: "No, I was merely in the portion of the rain that descended in my immediate vicinity."

He was so dumb that he thought "pitching woo" was a Chinese transfer student.

A freshman's father paid his son a surprise visit. Arriving at 1:00 AM, he banged on the fraternity house door.

A voice from the second floor yelled: "What do you want?"

"Does Harvey Chapman live here?" asked the father.

"Yeah," answered the voice, "bring him in."

One college freshman was so dumb that he stayed up all night studying for a blood test.

A father had been growing more and more exasperated because his college-age son persisted in borrowing his clothes. One evening the youth appeared dressed for a date.

"Isn't that my tie you're wearing, Edward?" the father asked sternly.

"Yes, Sir, I . . . I guess it is," said the son.

"And my shirt?"

"Yes, Sir."

"And my belt too!" the father exploded. "Will you kindly tell me what you're wearing that for?"

"Well, gee whiz, Dad," the son said defensively, "you don't want your pants to fall down, do you?"

Two coeds were discussing their social lives. One was a freshman, the other a senior.

The freshman asked her older friend, "What would you do if you'd had five dates with a fellow and he never even attempted to kiss you?"

The senior thought about it for a minute, then offered her advice, "Lie about it."

Nowadays the fellow who has the hardest time staying in college is the coach of a losing team.

Roomie: "Where did you catch your cold?"
Mark: "Reading on the porch of the dorm."
Roomie: "Man, it's cold out there, what were you doing out there?"
Mark: "Doing my outside reading."

A graduate student working on juvenile delinquency reported in a sociology seminar that he was having difficulty collecting data. His project was to telephone a dozen homes around 9 PM and ask the parents if they knew where their children were at that hour.

"My first five calls," he lamented, "were answered by children who had no idea where their parents were!"

A College Student's Letter to Her Parents

DEAR MOM AND DAD:

Everything is OK, well, almost everything—you see, I have a terrible headache about every half hour. I've been having this headache ever since I jumped from my dormitory during the fire. A fine looking young man was passing my window when he saw the flames leaping from the window. He was kind enough to call the fire department and ambulance. Since my furniture was burned up and my room destroyed, I have been staying at this young man's apartment. I thought seriously about marrying him but I know how you feel about mixed marriages.

Mom and Dad—none of the above happened to me. I don't have a headache. There was not a fire in the dorm

and I didn't meet a young man with whom I'm living.

I am writing this letter to tell you that I've just received my report card. I have three *D*'s and two *F*'s. I just thought, if I put this in a different perspective, it would sound better!

YOUR LOVING DAUGHTER

Credit

If you want a short winter, have your loan come due in the spring.

Salesclerk: "You make a small deposit, then pay no more for six months."
Customer: "Who told you about us?"

Always borrow money from a pessimist. He never expects to be repaid.

It's a world of credit we live in—swing now, pay later. A guy ran up a $1,500 bill on his Diners' Club card and charged it to his American Express account!

Isn't it incredible? Nowadays if someone gives you cash, you get suspicious. Maybe his credit is no good.

"I've come to pay that bill I've owed you for so long," said Jones. "That letter you wrote me would get money

out of a stone. How did you ever think it up?"

Replied his creditor: "I didn't. I selected the best parts from letters my son sends me from college."

Today we have the haves, the have-nots, and the charge-its.

I shop like a bull—charge everything.

Definitions

JOINT CHECKING ACCOUNT—A device that permits the wife to beat you to the draw.

THE WORLD'S BEST AFTER-DINNER SPEECH— "Waiter, give me both checks."

DEFEAT—One who has ulcers, but still isn't a success.

DIVORCE—A vow tied with a slipknot.

MASON AND DIXON LINE—The division between "You-all" and "Youse-guys."

COMMITTEE — A group of people who individually can do nothing and who collectively decide nothing can be done.

DANGER — To try to leap a chasm in two jumps.

FRUSTRATION — Buying a new boomerang and finding it impossible to throw the old one away.

HYPOCHONDRIAC — A man who can't leave being well enough alone.

AMERICA — A place where we jump traffic lights to save seconds and wait patiently for hours on the first tee.

AVERAGE — The best of the lousy and the lousiest of the best.

SUCCESS — The ability to make money enough to meet obligations you wouldn't have if you didn't make so much money.

BUDGET — Comes from the French word *bougette* which means a small bag, which is what the taxpayer is left holding.

CANCER — Cure for smoking.

TELEVISION ANNOUNCER — A person who talks until he gives you a headache and then tries to sell you something for it.

HANGOVER — The wrath of grapes.

CELEBRITY — A person who works hard all his life to become well known, then wears dark glasses to avoid being recognized.

EGOTIST — One who is always me-deep in conversation.

BACHELOR — One who never Mrs. a girl.

Determination

We don't fully realize the hardships of our pioneer ancestors until we remember that day after day they plodded their way westward into the setting sun without sunglasses.

A strong, stalwart Texan was unloading blacksmiths' anvils from a ship in a Houston port. The plank broke, and he fell into the water. He went down the first time and then the second time. Just before he went down the third time, he yelled, "If someone doesn't help me, I'm going to drop one of these anvils."

The baseball season was about over and the team was firmly entrenched in last place when the manager decided to let a rookie pitcher get a little major league experience. The rookie, who had more determination than skill, was in deep trouble before long. Finally the manager walked out to the mound and said, "Son, I think you have had enough for today."

"But I struck out this guy the last time he was up," the young hurler protested violently.

"I know," snapped the manager as he waved another pitcher in from the bullpen, "but that was earlier this inning."

They say there is a filling station down in Louisiana where the owner has a pot of strong chickory coffee brewing at all times.

One traveler reported that the operator demanded that he drink a cup of coffee before driving on.

"No, thank you," said the customer, "I don't drink coffee."

This seemed to enrage the operator of the station who promptly pulled out a gun and held it on the customer and said, "I said, drink a cup of my coffee."

After the obliging traveler had drunk a cup of coffee, the man handed him the gun and said, "Now hold the gun on me while I drink a cup."

Dieting

The family that eats together gets fat!

Linda: "You say you want to reduce? Why don't you try golf?"

Faye: "I tried that once, but it's no good. When I put the ball where I can see it, I can't hit it; and when I put it where I can hit it, I can't see it."

I know a man who is so fat that when he graduated from college they had to take an aerial photograph to get him in the picture.

A heavyset comedian complained, "I've been using artificial sweetener so long that I've gotten artificially fat."

Want to do some morning exercises? OK, up . . . down . . . up . . . down . . . up . . . down. Now the other lid.

Diets are for people who are thick and tired of it.

Doctor to portly patient: "Follow this diet, and in a couple of months I want to see three-fourths of you back here for a checkup."

The plump man and his wife were returning to their seats in the theater after intermission.

"Did I step on your toes as I went out?" he asked the man at the end of the row.

"You certainly did," exclaimed the man angrily, waiting for an apology.

"All right, Mary," said the fat man turning to his wife, "this is our row."

A woman got a look at her shadow on Groundhog Day and predicted six weeks of dieting.

A lady told her friend she wanted to go on a diet and asked for suggestions.

"I've heard of a wonderful new diet pill. You may eat all you can. It paralyzes your mouth and you can't eat!"

Farmers

He was preparing to go to the store and his wife told him to get a head of cabbage.

"What size?" he asked.

"Oh, about the size of your head," she told him.

On the way he met a friend who had a garden. "Just go over to my garden and take any head of cabbage you want," the friend offered generously.

Later, another friend asked the gardener, "What kind of idiot did you have walking in your garden? When I went by, he was trying his hat on one head of cabbage after another."

Two little boys from the country, visiting their grandmother, wandered down the street to inspect the new school that was just being finished. They found two electricians working in one of the rooms.

"What are you doing?" inquired one of the little visitors.

"We're just putting in the new electric switches, Sonny," replied one of the workmen.

"Man," said the other boy after a pause. "I'm sure glad we still have our old country school!"

A farmer who made it a rule to think before speaking was approached by a stranger one day and asked, "How much is that prize Jersey heifer of yours worth?"

The farmer thought a moment, then asked, "Are you the tax assessor or has she been run over by a truck?"

A farmer in the drought country was able to survive only because a kindly storekeeper gave him unlimited credit. Then came good fortune—plenty of rain and steadily rising prices for the farmer's crops. He paid back his entire debt, but the storekeeper didn't see him again for over a year.

The next time they met the farmer was driving a shiny new car and he and his four sons were dressed fit to kill. "How come you now shop elsewhere," asked the storekeeper reproachfully, "after I carried you on my books for so many lean years?"

The farmer all but wept. "Shucks, Tom," he drawled, "I didn't realize you sold for cash!"

Fishing

Tourist: "Good river for fish?"
Fisherman: "Must be, can't persuade any to come out."

"Say!" yelled the farmer, who owned a pond, "don't you see that sign: 'NO FISHING HERE'?"

"I sure do," said the disgusted fisherman. "The fellow that printed that sign really knew what he was talking about."

Lugging a huge fish, an angler met another fishing enthusiast whose catch consisted of twelve small fish.

"Howdy," said the first man as he gingerly laid down his fish and waited for comment.

The other fellow stared for a few moments and calmly responded, "Just caught the one, eh?"

A Texas fisherman was relating his efforts at catching a twenty-five-pound bass.

Friend: "Did it put up much of a fight?"

Texan: "Yep, but not half as much as the ten-pound grasshopper I caught it with."

Two men were fishing. Their luck was so good they were catching fish as never before. As the sun went down, one fisherman said to the other, "You'd better mark this place."

When they got to the pier, the first fisherman said to the second, "Did you mark the place?"

"Sure did, I put an *X* on the side of the boat just over the good spot."

"But," the first fisherman asked, "how do you know we can get the same boat tomorrow?"

A sad-looking little man had been waiting quite some time for his order to be filled. Finally a waiter appeared

and said, "Your fish will be coming in a few minutes now."

The customer brightened up a bit. "Tell me," he asked, "what bait are you using?"

An old-timer sat on the river bank, obviously awaiting a nibble, though the fishing season had not officially opened. The game warden stood behind him quietly for several minutes.

"You the game warden?" the old-timer inquired.

"Yep."

Unruffled, the old man began to move the fishing pole from side to side. Finally he lifted the line out of the water.

Pointing to a minnow wiggling on the end of the line, he said, "Just teaching him to swim."

Food

A corn syrup manufacturing company received the following letter: "Dear Sirs: I have ate three cans of your corn syrup and it has not helped my corns one bit."

Impatient diner: "Look here, Waiter, I ordered chicken pie, but there isn't a bit of chicken in it!"

Waiter: "That's all right, Sir. We also have cottage cheese but as far as I know, there're no cottages in it."

Camper: "How can I tell mushrooms from toadstools?"
Leader: "Eat some before you go to bed. If you wake up the next morning, they're mushrooms."

Two boys were walking down a street together. One boy was eating an apple.

The boy with no apple said to the boy with the apple, "If I had an apple, I would give it to you."

The boy with the apple said, "What are you kicking about — I have it, don't I?"

A woman missed her gloves as she was leaving the restaurant where she had dined with her husband. Asking him to wait, she hurried back to look for them, searching first on the table and finally peering under it.

The waiter who had served them hurried up to her. "Pardon me, Madam," he said, "but the gentleman is there by the door."

Customer in a Restaurant: "I'll have some raw oysters, not too small, not too salty, or too fat. They must be cold, and I want them quickly!"

Waiter: "Yes, Sir. With or without pearls?"

On the wharf in San Francisco a man walked into a restaurant and asked, "Do you serve crabs?" The waitress said quickly, "Sure, we serve anybody! Sit down!"

Waitress: "We have practically everything on the menu."

Diner: "So I see. Can you bring me a clean one?"

A boy's idea of a balanced meal is a piece of cake in each hand.

A man showed the doctor his wife's hand. "She did it preparing dinner," he explained. "It's frostbitten."

The other night I ordered a twenty-dollar dinner and the waiter asked, "On rye or white?"

Customer: "Waiter, this food is terrible. I want to talk to the owner of this restaurant!"

Waiter: "You can't. He's out to lunch."

A man walked into a fast-food restaurant and ordered a hamburger, french fries, and a Coke to go. The young man behind the counter noticed an unusual deformity. His customer's right arm was frozen in a circular position with his hand seemingly glued to his hip.

Risking goodwill, the young man asked, "Sir, I know it isn't polite to ask. However, I've never seen a deformity like yours. Could you please tell me what happened to your arm?"

The man looked quickly at his arm and exclaimed, "Oh no, I've dropped my watermelon!"

"I can't eat this garbage," cried the enraged diner. "Call the manager."

"It's no use," said the waiter. "He won't eat it either."

Jeff: "Do you think apples are as healthy as they say?"
Mike: "Never heard one complain."

A man dining in a restaurant found his steak very tough. In fact it was so tough that in spite of jabbing and stabbing he couldn't cut it at all.

At last he called the waiter to his table. "You'll have to take this steak back and get me another. It's so tough I can't cut it."

The waiter leaned over and looked at it closely. "I'm sorry, Sir, I can't take this steak back. You see, you've bent it rather badly."

Diner: "Waiter, my plate is damp."
Waiter: "Sorry, Sir. That's your soup."

Government

Who is a typical American? A typical American, says a congressman, is a man who has just driven home from an Italian movie in his German automobile, who is sitting on a Danish chair, drinking Brazilian coffee out of an English bone-china cup, writing a letter on Canadian-made paper with a Japanese ball-point pen to his congress-

man—complaining about too many foreign imports coming into the country.

A woman went into a small town post office recently and asked for five dollars worth of stamps.

"What denomination?" asked the clerk.

"Well," came the angry reply, "I didn't know it would ever come to this, but if the nosy government people have to know, I'm a Baptist!"

With modern medicine doing so well at increasing our life expectancy, we'd better be careful about adding to the national debt—we might have to pay it off ourselves, instead of passing it on.

"What's your job with the Federal government?"

"I'm in charge of keeping obsolete files up-to-date."

Every man needs a wife—because too many things go wrong that cannot be blamed on the government.

Hunting

A hunter hired a guide to lead him through the wilderness. The hunter soon discovered they were walking around in circles.

"We're lost," the hunter complained to the guide. "I

thought you said you were the best guide in the state of Maine."

"I am," said the guide. "But I think we're in Canada now."

A well-known American game hunter flew to New Guinea for some hunting. After two weeks he was captured by a tribe of head shrinkers. They held him captive for six months by which time everyone thought he was dead. Finally he managed to escape and make his way to town. First thing he did was to call his wife in California.

"Darling," she sobbed, "it's a miracle that you're alive. An absolute miracle! How are you?"

"I'm all right," the hunter explained, "except that I have no clothes. Would you please fly me some? I could use the following immediately: Three shirts size 15½, socks size 11½, shoes size 10C, and oh yes, I can use a hat here to protect my forehead."

"What size, Darling?"

"One and seven-eights."

A hunter from the city bagged a big buck deer. Just about that time, the game warden arrived and asked if the hunter had a hunting license.

The hunter said he didn't have a license, so the game warden had to take the hunter and the deer to town.

The game warden helped the hunter drag the 300-pound deer out to the road—at which point the hunter exclaimed, "I just remembered—I do have a deer license after all."

Husband and Wife

The minister asked for anyone who knew a truly perfect person to stand up. After a long pause a meek-looking fellow in the back stood. "Do you really know a perfect person?" he was asked.

"Yes, Sir, I do," answered the little man.

"Would you please tell the congregation who this rare, perfect person is?" pursued the preacher.

"Yes, Sir, my wife's first husband."

Gene: "They tell me your wife is outspoken."
Jewell: "By whom?"

A couple lived together for sixty years without a single argument — they shared the same hearing aid.

"My husband didn't leave a bit of insurance."

"Then where did you get that gorgeous diamond ring?"

"Well, he left a thousand dollars for a casket and five thousand dollars for a stone. This is the stone."

"What makes you think your wife is getting tired of you?"

"Every day this week she has wrapped my lunch in a road map!"

The reason most men don't bring the boss home for dinner is that she is already there!

Question: "Do you wake up grouchy every morning?"
Answer: "No, I just let her sleep and I go on to work."

"How do you want your eggs this morning?" an accommodating wife asked her grumpy husband.

"Scramble one and boil the other!" was his gruff reply.

She scrambled one and boiled the other and put them on his plate.

He looked up and exclaimed, "You scrambled the wrong one!"

One man said his wife reminded him of an angel—"She's always up in the air harping on something."

An exasperated husband came home from work to find his car had crashed through the house and was sitting in the living room. He was happy to learn that his wife wasn't injured.

He asked, "What happened?"

His wife replied, "I just drove into the kitchen and turned right."

Said Mrs. Thomas A. Edison: "I don't know what you're doing, Tom, but I can't sleep with that light on."

"This," said the salesman, holding up a royal blue, silk jacket, "is the very last word, just the thing for the man-about-town."

"I agree," the woman said, "But what do you have for a louse-around-the-house?"

She had been married four times. Her first husband was a banker, the second an actor, the third a minister, the fourth an undertaker. When asked why the different ones she said: "One for the money, two for the show, three to make ready, and four to go."

An experienced husband is one who remembers his wife's birthday but forgets which one it is.

A newcomer reports that before moving into a new house she and her husband put down an expensive vinyl floor, which they resolved to treat with tender, loving care. "Be careful of that floor, it's just been waxed," she warned the moving man.

"Don't worry, Lady," he said heartily, "I'm wearing spiked shoes."

He looked out of the window and called to his wife. "There goes that woman Bill Jones is in love with."

She dropped the cup she was drying in the kitchen, hurtled through the door, knocked over a lamp, and craned her neck to look. "Where?" she panted.

"There," he pointed, "that woman at the corner in the tweed coat."

"Oh, you," she said, "that's his wife!"

"Well, of course it is," he replied.

Mrs. Brown: "Whenever I'm in the dumps, I get myself a new hat."

Mrs. Jones: "I was wondering where you got them."

"I simply can't stand my husband's nasty disposition," wept the young bride. "Why, he's made me so jittery that I'm losing weight."

"Then why don't you leave him?" asked her aunt.

"Oh, I'm going to," the bride assured her. "I'm just waiting until he gets me down to 120 pounds."

"Why didn't you report the robbery at once?" an insurance agent asked a woman claimant. "Didn't you suspect something when you came home and discovered all the drawers opened and the contents scattered all over the room?"

"Not really," she replied. "I thought my husband had been looking for matching socks."

A henpecked husband visited a psychiatrist and said he had a recurring nightmare. "Every night," he said, "I dream I'm shipwrecked with twelve beautiful women."

"What's so terrible about that?" asked the psychiatrist.

"Have you ever tried cooking for twelve women?" said the browbeaten husband.

Why criticize your wife's judgment? Look who she married!

"Those are my husband's ashes in that beautiful vase on top of the TV."

"Indeed, I didn't know you were a widow."

"I'm not now, but I will be any day now if that lazy guy doesn't start looking for ashtrays."

On one of his rare trips to the city an old hillbilly was so fascinated by a large building's elevators that he stood a long time in front of one. An old lady, bent and shriveled, entered, a light flashed, and in an instant she was gone. Moments later the same door opened and out stepped an attractive young woman. Walking away sadly the hillbilly muttered, "I shoulda brung my wife."

"I just read in the paper," said a suburban housewife, "that Mrs. Castle has cremated her third husband."

Her friend, a spinster, shook her head sadly. "Isn't that always the way?" she demanded. "Some of us can't get one and others have husbands to burn."

Traffic Officer: "When I saw you come around that curve I said to myself, forty-five at least!"

Woman Driver: "Well, you're wrong. These glasses just make me look older."

"The doctor said that my wife and I need more exercise, so I've just bought myself a set of golf clubs," said Estep to his neighbor.

"That's good. And what have you bought for your wife?"

"A lawn mower."

Angry Wife: "That ten dollars that was in your pants pocket last night—did you steal it out of my purse this morning?"

At breakfast a singer who was nursing a terrific hang-over remarked to his wife that he had cut himself shaving. He was afraid he'd lost a good deal of blood.

"How can you tell?" asked the wife. "Do you feel weak?"

"I feel OK," said the singer. "But I looked in the mirror, and my eyes have cleared up."

My wife, like most wives, is a great driver. She gets into the car, makes a left turn, a right turn, then pulls out of the garage.

"They say he married her because her uncle left her a million dollars."

"Oh, I don't think he's that kind of boy. I think he'd have married her no matter who left it to her."

Mr. and Mrs. Appleton entered the dentist's office.

Mrs. Appleton said, "I want a tooth pulled. I don't want gas or novocaine because I'm in a terrible hurry. Just pull the tooth as quickly as possible."

"You certainly are a brave woman," said the dentist. "Now, show me which tooth it is."

Mrs. Appleton turned to her husband and said, "Open your mouth and show the dentist which tooth it is, Dear."

With his wife sick in bed, pandemonium reigned supreme in the kitchen. The tea was missing. He looked high and low and finally called to his wife, "I can't find the tea, Dear. Where do you keep it?"

"I don't know why you can't find it," came the peevish reply. "It's right in front, on the cupboard shelf, in a cocoa tin marked 'matches.' "

"Every time I ask you something," the angered husband said to his wife, "you answer all my questions with another question. Why?"

"Do I really do that?" the wife replied.

Judge: "You say your arrest was due to a misunderstanding?"

Prisoner: "Yes, your honor. My wife kept saying she wanted a mink stole for her birthday so I finally went out and stole one."

A wife bought a new wig and thought it would be a good joke to surprise her husband at the office. She walked in on him and asked: "Do you think you could find a place in your life for a woman like me?"

"Not a chance," he snapped. "You remind me too much of my wife."

During World War II a milk bottle was fished out of the Pacific Ocean. It contained a piece of water-soaked paper. The writing was too faint to be deciphered, so the FBI was called in.

Various tests were made, an array of acids applied. At last, six words stood out in startling clarity. They were, "Two quarts of milk, no cream."

Boy: If I had a million dollars, do you know where I'd be?"

Girl: "I sure do. You'd be on our honeymoon!"

Joe (to neighbor): "My wife spends so much money that it's driving me crazy."

Neighbor: "Why don't you talk to her about it?"

Joe: "Oh, it's easier to talk to the creditors."

Wife: "I think you might talk to me while I sew."

Hubby: "Why don't you sew to me while I read?"

Clerk: "The gown will be $200, Madam. I guarantee a fit."

Customer: "I, too, guarantee a fit when my husband learns the price."

Wife: "But, Darling, this isn't our baby."

Husband: "Keep quiet; it's a better buggy."

"There," said the newlywed husband pointing to Niagara Falls, "I told you that if you married me I'd show you the world's largest cataract."

"Cataract!" screamed the former chorus girl. "I thought you said Cadillac."

When I was first married, I'd come home and it was so peaceful. My little dog would race around barking at me, and my wife would bring me my slippers. Now, five years later, my dog brings the slippers and my wife barks.

My wife is a light eater; as soon as it's light out, she starts eating.

Judge: "How did you happen to hit the other car?"
Motorist: "It was entirely my wife's fault. She fell asleep in the backseat."

A henpecked husband was terribly disappointed when his wife gave birth to a baby girl.
He confided to a friend, "I was hoping for a boy to help me with the housework."

Pretty girl: "May I try on that two-piece suit in the window?"
Store manager: "Go right ahead. It might help business."

He: "Did anyone ever tell you how wonderful you are?"
She: "I don't believe they ever did."
He: "Then where'd you ever get the idea?"

I'd like to tell you about my wife. It takes her forty-five minutes to put on her lipstick. The reason is, she's got a big mouth.

"But why," demanded the puzzled judge of the burglar standing before, "did you break into the same store three nights running?"

"Well, Judge, it's like this," was the reply. "I picked out a dress for my wife and I had to change it twice."

Two political candidates were having a hot debate. Finally one of them jumped up and yelled at the other: "What about the powerful interests that control you?"

The other guy screamed back, "You leave my wife out of this."

Woman, fishing: "Have you another cork, Dear? This one keeps sinking."

I just bought my wife a second car — a tow truck.

A man accompanied a friend home for dinner one evening and noticed that as soon as they entered the door, his friend kissed his wife and told her how pretty she looked. After dinner he complimented his wife on the food and kissed her again.

"Do you always do that?" asked the visitor when they were alone.

"You bet I do," answered the man. "It helps keep our marriage a happy one."

The visitor was greatly impressed and decided to use the same procedure with his own wife. That night he swept her into his arms when he got home and kissed her warmly. "Sweetheart," he said, "you look wonderful tonight, and I'm a lucky man to have such a beautiful wife."

His wife looked at him in amazement, then burst into tears.

"For Pete's sake," exclaimed the astonished man, "what's the matter?"

"What a day this has been!" his wife answered. "First Johnny sprained his ankle, then the washing machine broke down and flooded the basement, and now you come home drunk!"

She: He pays so little attention to me that if I died I don't think he'd be able to identify the body.

My wife sure is immature. Every time I take a bath, she comes in and sinks my boats.

A young housewife got fed up with the voluminous correspondence and complicated forms she found herself involved in whenever a mail-order item was unsatisfactory. So when her iron went bad, she simply sent it back with the manufacturer's tag, on which she had printed crudely: "My Iron, She No Get Hot.'

Without further ado she received a new iron.

An excited woman called police to report an auto accident.

Asked where it happened, she said, "I don't have time to talk now. I'll tell you when you get here."

Then she hung up.

"Hey, you! Pull over!" shouted the traffic cop. The lady complied, and the judge next day fined her twenty-five dollars. She went home in great anxiety lest her husband, who always examined her checkbook, should learn of the incident. Then inspiration struck and she marked the check stub, "One pullover, $25."

Harried motorist, teaching his wife to drive: "Go on green, stop on red, careful on amber, and look out when I turn white."

An elderly woman was driving along in her Volkswagen when the motor sputtered. She pulled to a halt on the side of the road, got out, and looked under the hood.

Several minutes later another woman stopped her Volkswagen and asked if she could be of help.

The perplexed owner looked from under the hood and said, "It seems I don't have a motor."

The second woman politely answered, "I've got an extra one in the trunk you can have."

Inflation

Secretary (on phone): "He's gone to Washington to get a government loan to pay back what he borrowed from the bank to pay his income tax."

A bum helped a Scout across the road. When he got him to the other side, the Scout said, "Here's something for a cup of coffee" as he pressed a small wad of something into the bum's hand. It was a piece of sugar.

If your outgo exceeds your income, then your upkeep will be your downfall.

"May I have some stationery?" a man asked the hotel clerk.

"Are you a guest of the hotel?" asked the clerk.

"No, I'm paying sixty dollars a day," said the man.

Write something that will live forever—sign a house mortgage.

"Three meals a day, a roof over my head, two cars, a boat, a power mower, and a contented wife—why shouldn't I be in debt?"

My wife found a new way to save her money—she uses mine.

Another thing we hate about inflation is that it didn't hit years ago when prices were lower.

Insurance

Friends were comforting the widow of a tugboat skipper who had recently drowned.

"You poor dear," said one. "I hope you were left with something."

"Oh, yes," said the widow, "Two hundred thousand dollars."

"Imagine that. And he couldn't even read or write."

The widow nodded earnestly and added, "Or swim."

I have a great insurance man. He just sold me a policy that gives me $5,000 if I'm strangled, $10,000 if I die in a submarine, and $200,000 if I die in an accident. Think how well off I'd be if I were accidentally strangled to death in a submarine! He also sold me a policy that pays me $50 a week for life if I live longer than 90 years. That's so I won't be a burden to my mother and father.

After buying a $50,000 insurance policy before a plane trip, the traveler stepped on a nearby scale. Out came one of those fortune-telling cards. The message read, "A recent investment may pay big dividends."

"Why in the world did you write a policy on a man ninety-eight years old?" asked the indignant insurance inspector.

"Well," explained the new agent, "I looked in the census report and found that only a few people that age die each year!"

An insurance salesman was getting nowhere in his efforts to sell a policy to a farmer. "Look at it this way," he said finally. "How would your wife carry on if you should die?"

"Well," answered the farmer reasonably, "I don't

reckon that's any concern o' mine — so long as she behaves herself while I'm alive."

A cowpuncher had applied for a policy, and the insurance agent was quizzing him. "Have you ever met with any accidents?"

"No," said the cowboy, but added, in an effort to be helpful, "A bronc kicked two of my ribs in last summer, and a couple years ago a rattlesnake bit me on the ankle."

"And don't you call those accidents?"

"Naw," replied the cowboy. "They done it a-purpose."

Lawyers

Son: "Daddy, why is a man only allowed one wife?"

Father: "Son, when you grow older you will understand that the law protects those who are unable to protect themselves."

An ambitious lawyer, wanting to impress a prospective client with his importance and wealth, buzzed his secretary on the intercom.

"Miss Collins," he barked, "get me my broker."

"Which one," came the reply, "stock or pawn?"

The prosecuting attorney asked the chief witness, "Aren't you a barber by trade?"

The witness replied arrogantly, "I am a tonsorial artist."

"Well, now," interjected the judge, "isn't that splitting hairs?"

84

A doctor was fuming when he finally reached his table at a banquet after breaking away from a woman who sought his advice on a health problem. "Do you think I should send her a bill?" he asked a lawyer who was sitting next to him.

"Why not?" the lawyer replied. "You rendered professional services by giving advice."

"Thanks," the physician said. "I think I'll do that."

When the doctor went to his office the next day to send a bill to the annoying woman, he found a statement from the lawyer. It read: "For legal services—$25.

"What is that little boy crying about?" the benevolent old lady asked of the ragged urchin.

"That other kid swiped his candy," he said.

"But how is it that you have the candy now?"

"Sure I have the candy now. I'm the other kid's lawyer."

"Do you have a criminal lawyer in town?" a tourist asked an old-timer.

"Well, we think so," the old man said, "but we can't prove it."

Laziness

If some men's ships did come in, they'd be too lazy to unload them.

A farmer put up this sign at the entrance of his pasture: "Hunters, please don't shoot anything on my place that isn't moving. It might be my new hired hand."

"How is that new man you hired? Is he a steady guy?"
"Yes, so far he has been practically motionless."

If you know anything about the speed of light, you'll agree that it gets here too early in the morning.

A sailor in a good mood entered the barracks and called out, "I'll give a dollar to the laziest man here."
Everyone scrambled to his feet and rushed forward to tell how lazy he was except one tall Texan. He drawled, "Just roll me over and slip it in my pocket."

A foreman caught one of his men with his eyes closed, but he had to admit the fellow's excuse was a new one. "What's the matter," the man wanted to know, "can't a guy say a prayer once in a while?"

Marriage

You don't know what you're missing, unless you've attended a modern Japanese wedding. Instead of rice they throw transistor radios at the newlyweds.

When the widow appeared at the attorney's office and learned that her recently departed spouse had left most of his fortune to a Broadway chorus girl, she grew livid with rage.

Off she raced to the cemetery, where she demanded that the inscription on her husband's tombstone be changed immediately. The manager explained that such a change was impossible, that the inscription "Rest in Peace" would have to remain.

"OK," said the wife indignantly. "But underneath that line add the words, 'Until we meet again.' "

Woman to Marriage Counselor: "That's my side of the story—now let me tell you his."

A father turned to his daughter and said: "Your young man approached me this afternoon and asked for your hand and I consented."

"But, Father," cried the daughter, "I don't want to leave Mother."

"I quite understand," he said. "But don't let me stand in the way of your happiness—take your mother with you."

It was a teenage marriage. She was fifteen. He was sixteen. Both families disapproved, but they attended the wedding. As the preacher asked the bridegroom to repeat after him, "With all my worldly goods I thee endow," the groom's mother said to her husband, "There goes his paper route."

His mother playfully asked seven-year-old Timmy about the little neighbor girl, a newcomer to the block.

Timmy replied that he intended to marry her.

"And where will you go for your honeymoon?" she asked.

Came the immediate answer: "Disneyland!"

The bridegroom was in a poetic frenzy as he strolled along the seashore. "Roll on, thou deep and dark blue ocean, roll on," he recited to his happy bride.

"Oh, Gerald," she exclaimed, "how wonderful you are; it's doing it!"

A well-known executive, also well-known as a ladies' man, announced at the club that his wife had just hired a new secretary for him.

"Is that so?" responded a friend. "Blonde or brunette?"

"Neither," replied the executive sadly, "he's bald."

It's true, we fight. But we've never gone to bed mad. Of course, one year we were up for three months.

Marriage would work out better if both sides would operate on a thrifty-thrifty basis.

The young man approached his lady love's brother in a dither of excitement. "Guess what, Jimmy," he exclaimed, "your sister and I are going to be married!"

"Huh!" said the youngster, unimpressed. "Are you just now finding out?"

Girls tend to marry men like their fathers, say psychologists. Is that why mothers cry at weddings?

A Coed Prayed: "Dear Lord, I'm not asking just for myself, but please give my mother a son-in-law."

If you have half a mind to get married, do it. That's really all it takes.

Bride to New Husband: "There you are, Darling, my first meal cooked just the way you'd better like it."

Adam and Eve had an ideal marriage. He didn't have to hear about all the men she could have married — and she didn't have to hear about the way his mother cooked.

A WEDDING RING — tourniquet worn on one's finger to stop circulation.

A HONEYMOON — the brief period between "I do" and "You'd better."

Medical

An Alaskan on arriving in Texas approached a bystander and asked, "Where can I find a doctor?"

"Are you ill?" inquired the Texan.

"No," grinned the Alaskan, "I'm suffering from claustrophobia."

A customer returned to his favorite druggist. "And how did you like the bath salts?" asked the druggist.

Said the customer ruefully, "They tasted good enough but frankly, I don't think they have the same effect as a real bath."

Saint Peter (to new arrival): "How'd you get here?"
Guest: "Flu."

A pharmacist left his drugstore to go eat lunch. To his teenage helper he said, "You watch the store for a few minutes while I'm away."

The phone rang in a few minutes. The young man picked up the phone and said, "Hello."

"Can you fill a prescription for sulfa drugs and penicillin?" inquired the caller.

The young man paused and answered, "When I said 'Hello,' I told you all I know."

In the old days a man worked on and on. He had tired blood but didn't know it.

Did you hear about the second-grader who just had school dental inspection? His group had 20 percent fewer teeth.

I use an electric toothbrush. Now I see my electrician twice a year.

"I'm getting really worried, Doctor, about myself. I need something to stir me up, something to take me out of my state of lethargy, and put me in fighting trim. Have you included anything like that in this prescription?"

"No, not in the prescription. You'll find that in the bill."

"What are you doing for your cold, Joe?"

"Coughing," answered Joe.

"No, no, I mean, what are you taking for it?"

"Make me an offer!"

Many a person gets a bad liver from being a bad liver.

Patient: "My ear rings all the time. What can I do?"

Doctor: "Get an unlisted ear."

A Medicare patient awoke after surgery to find a sign propped up against his incision. It read, "This is a Federal project showing your tax dollars at work."

"Socialized medicine," the youngster answered to a question on her test, "is when grown-ups get together and talk about their operations."

"A bad cold is both positive and negative. Sometimes the eyes have it, sometimes the nose."

Surgeons invited to dinner parties are often asked to carve the meat, or, worse yet, to watch the host carve while commenting on the surgeon's occupation. At one party a surgeon was watching the carving while his host kept up a running commentary. "How am I doing, Doc? How do you like that technique, I'd make a pretty good surgeon — don't you think?"

When the host finished and the slices of meat lay neatly on the serving tray, the surgeon spoke up, "Anybody can take them apart, Harry. Now let's see you put them back together again."

"I'm Doctor Hamilton's nurse," a sweet voice announced to a well-known Hollywood writer, "and the reason I'm phoning you, Sir, is that your check came back."

"Just tell the doctor," the writer answered, "so did my arthritis."

Doctor: "You're coughing more easily today."
Patient: "I should be, I've been practicing all night."

Patient: "Why are the shades down, Doctor?"
Doctor: "There's a big fire across the street. I didn't want you to come out of the anesthesia and think the operation had been a failure."

92

A doctor advised, "I can't do anything for your problem — it's hereditary."

"Then send the bill to my father, will you, Doc?"

A young mother, paying a visit to her doctor, was making no attempt to restrain her five-year-old son who was ransacking an adjoining treatment room.

Finally an extra loud clatter of bottles did prompt her to say, "I hope you don't mind Johnny being in your examination room, Doctor."

"Not at all," said the doctor calmly. "He'll quiet down in a moment when he gets to the poison cabinet."

A young medical student was called to the dean's office. "Son," advised the dean, "you're doing pretty well here at school, but you must learn to write a little less clearly."

Leroy: "I keep seeing spots before my eyes."
Betty: "Have you seen a doctor?"
Leroy: "No, just spots."

Have you heard about the tree surgeon who fell out of his patient?

"Well, Doc, you sure kept your promise when you said you would have me walking again in a month."

"Well, well, that's fine."

"Yes, I had to sell my car when I got your bill."

Today medicine is very specialized — I had a head cold, and when it went to my chest I had to change doctors.

A doctor was called to the bedside of a millionaire. "Madame," he said to the millionaire's wife after the examination, "I don't like the looks of your husband at all."

"I know, I know," said the wife. "But really, he's very good to the children."

A forgetful patient went to a doctor for a check-up. The doctor wrote out a prescription in his usual illegible writing. The patient put it in his pocket and forgot to have it filled. Every morning for two years he showed it to the conductor as a railroad pass. Twice it got him into Radio City Music Hall, once into the baseball park, and once into the symphony. He got a raise from the cashier by showing it as a note from the boss. One day he mislaid it at home and his daughter picked it up, played it on the piano, and won a scholarship to a conservatory of music.

The army doctor wanted to be sure that the newly enlisted man was perfectly normal. Suspiciously he said:

"What do you do for your social life?"

"Oh," the man blushed, "I just sit around mostly."

"Hmmm — never go out with girls?"

"Nope."

"Don't you even want to?"

The man was uneasy. "Well, yes, sort of."

"Then, why don't you?"

"My wife won't let me, Sir."

The telephone in the doctor's home rang at 3 AM.

"What do you charge for a house call?" the caller asked.

"Twenty-five dollars," the doctor mumbled sleepily.

"And how much for an office visit?"

"Fifteen dollars."

"All right," the caller said quickly. "I'll meet you at your office in ten minutes."

An old doctor in a small town finally took a vacation. He assigned his youngest son, not long out of medical school, to look after his practice. When the father returned, he asked his son if anything unusual had happened in his absence.

"I cured that indigestion Mrs. Framston had been suffering from for thirty years," the son proudly announced.

His father stormed, "That indigestion put you through prep school, college, and medical school."

Ministers

A minister who always read his sermons, placed his manuscript on the pulpit about half an hour before the service. One young member of his congregation removed the last page.

Preaching vigorously, the minister came to the words, "So Adam said to Eve . . ." Turning the page, he was horrified to discover the final page was missing. As he shuffled through the other pages, he gained a little time by repeating, "So Adam said to Eve . . ."

Then in a low voice, which the microphone carried to every part of the church, he added, "There seems to be a leaf missing."

A member of the Billy Graham team was meeting with the local pastors planning a Billy Graham crusade. As the subject of the offering came up, one pastor stood and said, "We don't need to worry about the offering because the Bible says that the cattle on a thousand hills belong to the Lord."

A Billy Graham associate replied, "The cattle on a thousand hills *do* belong to the Lord. However, those cattle need some cowboys to get out there and get them."

The pastor was baptizing some new adult converts. As one lady came up out of the water, she exclaimed to the congregation, "Bless the Lord, O my soul."

The next convert exclaimed, "The Lord is my shepherd."

The third quoted the verse, "I can do all things through Christ."

Since the fourth one to be baptized was a man with very little Bible knowledge who had a bad case of stage fright, he came up out of the water, grinned at the congregation, and exclaimed, "Merry Christmas, everyone!"

A pastor came into his pulpit one Sunday morning with a large bandage on his chin. Before reading his text, he explained his injury. "I had my mind on my sermon this morning while shaving and cut my chin."

After a long sermon, one of his members remarked, "He should have kept his mind on his chin and cut the sermon."

A new pastor explained to his congregation his first Sunday, "I have a technique for remembering names. I try to associate the person's name with another rhyming word."

After the morning service, he met Mrs. Womack. "Ah, your name will be easy to remember," he said. "I'll just think of your name and then think of stomach — Womack and stomach — they rhyme."

On the following Sunday morning, the pastor shook Mrs. Womack's hand after the morning service and said, "Good morning, Mrs. Kelly."

A pastor wired all his pews with electricity. One Sunday from his pulpit he said, "All who will give $100 toward the new building, stand up." He touched a button and twenty people sprang up.

"Fine, fine," the preacher beamed. "Now all who will give $500, stand up." He touched another button and twenty more jumped to their feet.

"Excellent," he shouted. "Now all who will give $1,000, stand up." He threw the master switch and electrocuted fourteen deacons.

A preacher who suffered extremely strained relations with his congregation was finally appointed chaplain at the state prison. Elated to be rid of him so easily, the people came in great numbers to hear his farewell discourse. The pastor chose as his text, "I go and prepare a place for you . . . that where I am, there ye may be also" (John 14:3).

The minister of a small church believed some practical joker was joshing him as I.O.U.'s began to appear in the collection plate. But one Sunday night weeks later, the collection included an envelope containing bills equal to the total of the I.O.U.'s.

After that, the parson could hardly wait to see what amount the anonymous donor had promised. The range in contributions was from five to fifteen dollars, apparently based on what the donor thought the sermon to be worth. One Sunday the collection plate brought a note reading, "U.O.Me $5."

A burglar entered a minister's house at midnight. Drawing his weapon, he said, "If you stir, you're a dead man. I'm hunting for your money."

"Let me get up and turn on the light," said the minister, "and I'll hunt with you."

A certain church found itself burdened with a very tedious, pious, and self-centered pastor for a couple of years. Then came the day when he was called to another church. He announced his resignation by saying, "Brethren, the same Lord who sent me to you is now calling me away."

There was a moment's silence and suddenly the congregation rose as one and began to sing, "What a Friend We Have in Jesus."

The Baptist minister had been summoned to the bedside of a Presbyterian woman who was quite ill. As he went up the walk, he met the little daughter and said to her, "I'm very glad your mother remembered me in her illness. Is your minister out of town?"

"No," answered the child. "He's at home, but we thought it might be something contagious, and we didn't want to expose him to it."

A minister decided he would use his CB radio as a "witnessing tool." He, therefore, decided that he would give himself the handle of *Ichthus*. He reasoned that when someone would ask him for the meaning of his handle, he would explain that *Ichthus* is the Greek word for fish. Each of the Greek letters form an acrostic which means, "Jesus Christ, God's Son, Savior."

At the end of his first conversation on his first night out on the new CB, the minister signed off by saying, "This is Ichthus, and I'll be 10-10 on the side."

A trucker's nasal voice came back, "Good buddy, what did you say your handle was?"

"Ichthus," replied the preacher.

"Ichthus?" questioned the trucker, "what in the world is an Ichthus?"

The preacher replied, "Well, *Ichthus* is the Greek word for fish and the Greek word for fish forms an acrostic which means Jesus Christ, God's Son, Savior."

There was a long pause and then the trucker came back and said, "Did you say *Ichthus* was the Greek word for fish?"

"Yes," said the minister.

"Mercy sakes, Good Buddy," replied the trucker, "Why don't you just call yourself Fish?"

Misfortune

In every crowd, there is a hard-luck-Harry type of person who has had more troubles than all of his friends combined. For the first time, here is his story in print.

My Family and Friends

"I was born at a very early age."

"My foster parents put me up for adoption and I was adopted by a Korean family."

"When I was a boy my rocking horse died."

"My parents always pulled tricks on me. I came home from school in the second grade and found that they had moved."

"We were so poor that the mice in our house ate out."

"You've heard of powdered milk—we had powdered water."

"My girl friend was so ugly that she came in second in a beauty contest and she was the only contestant."

"I had an uncle who stole anything. He had rubber pockets so he could steal soup."

"I had a brother who fell into a lens grinding machine and made a spectacle of himself."

"We were so poor I was made in Japan."

"I was so poor I would trap sparrows on the roof, dip them in peroxide, and sell them as canaries."

My Hometown

"My hometown was so small that we didn't have a town drunk; we just took turns."

"It was so little that if there weren't a traveler passing through, the newspaper editor had to write articles about himself."

"My hometown was so small we didn't have gossip because it would have had to be either about the person who was telling or the one who was listening."

"My hometown was so small the local Howard Johnson's had only one flavor. Saturday nights we used to go down to the hotel to see who rented the room."

"The town where I came from was so small the fire department had an answering service and the police department had an unlisted number."

"My hometown was so small that when we had a

parade there was no one to watch it because everybody was in it."

"My hometown was so small that if we wanted entertainment we had to drive over to the next town and watch their stop light change because we didn't even have an intersection of our own."

My Early Life

"The school I went to had thirty-seven students, me and thirty-six Indians. One time we had a school dance, and it rained for thirty-six days straight."

"We fought the war on poverty long before the president thought of it. We lost. Actually, we were prisoners of war."

"To tell the truth I was the first grade-school dropout they ever had. I even flunked school bus."

"I once decided to be a poet. But after I wrote my first poem, I decided that I was in the wrong field. My poem went like this:

There was an old lady from my town
My, how she could mash potatoes
But she fell in love with a horse and buggy
Come, let us lean on the river.

"I used to cut classes from correspondence school—I sent in empty envelopes."

"When I was a small kid, our bathroom caught fire. But we were lucky, it didn't reach the house."

My Kind of Luck

"For a while I had a series of very unusual jobs. I was night watchman in a day camp, a deckhand on a submarine, a traffic director in a phone booth, a cruise director on a Ferris wheel."

"Things happen to me that never happened to anyone else. I bought a set of snow tires and they melted."

"I had a nose job and my nose grew back."

"My dad called me into the den one day and said, 'Hey, come here.' He always called me 'Hey.' He said, 'Why don't you go out and learn a trade so I'll know what kind of job you're out of,' which is an unkind thing to say to a sensitive boy of twenty-nine. So, to make him proud of me, I took the civil-service exam to be a mailman. The first question on the examination was, 'How far is it from the earth to the moon?' — so I figured, if that's the route they're going to give me, forget it. I don't want the job anyway."

"I'm the kind of person who, if it were raining soup, I'd be standing there with a fork."

"I've got the meanest wife in the world. If Moses had

ever met her, he would have written another command-
ment."

"I am also a highly regarded inventor. Among my
more famous inventions are a square bathtub which cannot leave a ring, artificial false teeth, and an imitation
Cadillac."

Money

The Internal Revenue Service was baffled by a letter
from a man who explained that he hadn't been able to
sleep well since 1970 when he cheated on his income tax.
Enclosed in the letter were five $100 bills.

The man concluded the letter by saying that if he
didn't sleep better now, he would send the rest.

My wife, a woman whom I adore,
Thinks $3.95 is far less than $4.00
What is priced at $4.00 she would think
    outrageous
If she saw the ad in the paper's pageous,
But at $3.95 she would likely feel
The item a bargain, an outright steal.
This five-cent saving delights my wife —
And has kept me poor all our married life.

A little boy said to his mother, "I'd rather have a million friends than a million dollars."

"Why?" asked his mother.

"Well, I figure it this way, if I get in trouble, they ought to be able to pitch in at least a dollar apiece to help me."

Three boys were bragging about their dads.

"My dad writes a couple of lines," the first boy said, "calls it a poem, and gets fifty dollars for it."

"My dad makes dots on paper, calls it a song," the second said, "and gets seventy-five dollars for it."

"That's nothing," said the third boy. "My dad writes a sermon on a sheet of paper, gets up in the pulpit, and reads it; and it takes four men to bring the money in."

A prominent Houston oilman caught his seven-year-old son lighting a cigarette with a thousand-dollar bill.

"How many times," the enraged father shouted, "have I told you — you're too young to smoke."

The two Texans emerged from their swanky private club on a rainy day to go back to their offices. Unable to get a taxi, they took refuge from the weather at an automobile dealer's showroom next door.

"There's no sense waiting any longer for a cab, I'll buy us a car," said the one Texan to the other.

"No, let me," his friend replied, "you bought lunch."

A Texas millionaire reported to police that his Cadillac had gone out of control and smashed half a dozen cars before it could be stopped. Fortunately, he added, the accident happened in his own garage.

A young woman reports she is putting all her money in taxes because it's the only thing sure to go up.

"My boy," said the father kindly, "don't you want to succeed in life as I did?"

"Well, I don't know," the son replied, slowly. "You were raised in the country and worked and scrimped so you could go to the city. Then you slaved to own a house in the city. Then you about killed yourself so you could buy this house in the country. I think I'm better off staying here than killing myself making that round trip."

Balancing your budget gets worse each year. These days you just can't reconcile your net income with your gross habits.

The preacher was outlining the service to the organist. "And when I get through with my sermon, I'll ask those of the congregation who want to contribute toward the mortgage to stand up. At this time, you play the appropriate music."

"What do you mean, 'appropriate music'?" asked the organist.

"The 'Star Spangled Banner,' of course," he replied.

A miser who had worn the same hat for fifteen years decided with a heavy heart that it was time to buy a new one.

Going into the only hat shop in the neighborhood, he said to the clerk: "Well, here I am again."

A group of wealthy businessmen were trying to help an old friend who had been persistently unlucky. Knowing that he was too proud to accept money as a gift, they rigged up a bogus raffle. Then they called at his dilapidated apartment and told him that they would all draw slips from a hat, and that the man who drew 4 would get $1,000. To make sure he would win, they wrote 4 on every slip.

After drawing, the conspirators glanced at their slips, crumpled them up, and waited for their friend to announce that he had the lucky number. But the fellow never opened his mouth. Finally, unable to bear the suspense, they asked him what number he had drawn from the hat.

"Six and seven eights," he answered glumly.

What a good many people are looking for is less to do, more time to do it in, and more pay for not getting it done.

With so much talk these days about inflation, some Chinese restaurant is going to serve "misfortune cookies."

I never worry. I've got enough money to last me the rest of my life — unless I buy something.

After a five-day blizzard, a Red Cross rescue team was carried by helicopter to a mountain cabin nearly covered with snow drifts. After knocking on the door, one rescuer stepped in and said, "We're from the Red Cross."

"Well," said the mountaineer, scratching his head, "it's been a tough winter and I don't see how we can give anything this year."

There are so many labor-saving devices on the market today that a man has to work all his life to pay for them.

An Indian chief, head of a tribe in Nevada, drove into Las Vegas for a little gambling. He ran into a bad streak and was wiped out. He thereupon climbed to the top of Mount Charleston and sent smoke signals to his tribe, asking for more money.

The tribe signaled back, "For what reason do you need money?"

Before the chief could reply a group of scientists from the Atomic Energy Commission detonated an atomic charge in the desert. A tremendous mushroom of smoke rose from the earth, darkening the sky.

Promptly, the tribe signaled, "All right, all right, sending money. Just don't holler."

The major problem with fund raising in any organization—"the shell-out falter."

The endless task of every family—trying not to have too much month left at the end of a paycheck.

A teenager was enthusiastically describing her new boy friend to her father.

"He sounds very nice, Dear," said the father, "but does he have any money?"

"Oh, you men are all alike," answered the girl. "Bob asked me the same thing about you."

Music

At the conclusion of a concert two ushers were applauding harder than anybody else. People seated nearby smiled appreciatively at the two music lovers—until one of them stopped applauding and the other one was heard to say, "Keep clapping. One more encore and we're on overtime."

Tenant: "The people upstairs are getting on my nerves. Why just last night they stamped and banged on the floor after midnight."

Landlord: "Did they awaken you?"

Tenant: "No. As it happened, I was still up practicing on my tuba."

I once sang for the king of Siam. At least he told me he was. He said, "Honey, if you're a singer, I'm the king of Siam."

Judge: "It seems to me that I have seen you before."

Prisoner: "You have. I gave your daughter singing lessons."

Judge: "Thirty years!"

To prove the belief that music charms the savage beast, a noted violinist journeyed into the heart of the African jungle. As he sat in a clearing, a gorilla, a boa constrictor, and a mean bull elephant approached. The musician played on his violin, and all three stopped motionless to listen to the tunes.

A snarling lion then crashed through the thicket with one leap, reached the violinist, and tore him to shreds.

The elephant remonstrated with the savage lion, demanding to know how come he had destroyed the man who played such sweet music.

"I can't hear you," said the lion.

Clyde: "You mean your teacher said your singing was 'heavenly'?"

Craig: "Well, practically that. He said it was 'unearthly'."

After dinner one evening a rancher's wife was entertaining their house guest by playing the piano. At one point she turned to the visitor and said, "I understand you love music."

"Yes," murmured the guest politely. "But never you mind. Keep right on playing."

The doorbell rang and the lady of the house discovered a workman, complete with tool chest, on the front porch.

"Madam," he announced, "I'm the piano tuner."

The lady exclaimed, "Why, I didn't send for a piano tuner."

The man replied, "I know you didn't, but your neighbors did."

Why do I sing so well in the shower and so badly at the recital?

When a conductor took his orchestra on a tour, he found this note under his hotel room door one night, "I think you should know that the fellow in your band who plays the instrument that pulls in and out only bothered playing during the odd moments you were looking straight at him."

Optimism—Pessimism

One rainy night in New York when there were no taxis to be had, a man started down the stairs of the Times Square subway. Halfway down he slipped, a stout lady toppled against him, and they ended up on the bottom step with the lady sitting in his lap. He tapped her briskly on the shoulder. "I'm sorry, Madam," he rasped, "but this is as far as I go."

Nothing is all wrong. Even a clock that has stopped running is right twice a day.

A fellow who made a point of never being pessimistic had a blind date with a very fat girl. As he took her home, he was trying to think of something optimistic to say when he left her. He stumbled around and finally come up with these words, "Lucy Mae, you sweat less than any fat girl I've ever met."

Two men jumped off a twelve-story building. One was an optimist, the other was a pessimist.

As they passed the fifth floor, the pessimist was overheard to say, "Help!"

The optimist yelled, "So far, so good."

OPTIMIST — a man who thinks the dry cleaners are shrinking the waistband of his trousers.

Two shoe salesmen were sent to Africa and South America.

The pessimist in Africa wrote back, "I'm coming back home. Nobody wears shoes here."

The optimist in South America wrote back, "Nobody wears shoes here. Send me some help."

Cowpoke: "How much are your spurs?"

Clerk: "Ten dollars a pair."

Cowpoke: "Here's five dollars, give me one."

Clerk: "What can you do with one spur?"

Cowpoke: "Well, I reckon if I get one side of the horse going, the other side will keep up."

A pessimistic fellow read his horoscope, which said: "Make new friends and see what happens." He went out, made three new friends, and nothing happened. Now he complains that he's stuck with three new friends.

People are funny. Tell a man there are 735,688,412,564 stars in the universe and he'll believe you. But when the same man sees a sign reading "Wet Paint," he'll stop and make a personal investigation.

A pessimist is a man who, when he smells flowers, looks around for a casket.

A pessimist thinks the world is against him — and it is.

A pessimist is somebody whose daydreams are nightmares.

Police

Helping the bruised man up from the pavement, the policeman said, "Can you describe the man who hit you?"
"That's what I was doing," was the answer, "when he hit me."

A man walked down the sidewalk dragging a chain. A policeman stopped him and asked, "What in the world are you doing dragging a chain down the street?"
"Have you ever heard of pushing one?" asked the strange pedestrian.

Crime in New York City has gone way down now that they've stationed a policeman in each subway station. So far not one train has been stolen.

Policeman: "Little boy, why do you keep running around the block?"

Little Boy: "I'm running away from home, but I'm not allowed to cross the street by myself."

On his first day out, a rookie policeman was having trouble with a bum. The derelict swung at him and knocked him down. Another policeman, seeing the commotion from across the street, started over to help. But as he approached, the rookie scrambled to his feet and started to run. The other officer finally caught him and demanded, "What's the matter with you anyway?"

"Holy suffering!" panted the new recruit. "I forgot I was a policeman. In the neighborhood where I grew up we always ran from cops!"

Politics

A sidewalk interviewer asked a retired man what he thought of the two candidates for an election.

"When I look at them," the retired man replied, "I'm thankful only one of them can get elected."

When an office holder in Washington died, a perennial office seeker hurried to the White House to tell the president that he'd like to "take the deceased man's place." The president answered, "If it's all right with the undertaker, it's all right with me."

There is no life on the moon. You can bet your last dollar on it. If there were life, the people there would have requested U.S. aid long before now.

"And now, gentlemen," continued the congressman, "I wish to tax your memories."

"Gracious," muttered a colleague, "why haven't we thought of that before?"

Nowadays one has to be very careful with political jokes because many times political jokes get elected.

The senator had injured his eye while on summer vacation and his doctor treated it, making a patch for him to wear over the hurt eye.

"You'd better wear this patch whenever you are exposed to a strong wind," the doctor said.

"Guess you'd better put it on me now," said the senator. "I'm due on the Senate floor right away."

Voter: "Why, I wouldn't vote for you if you were Saint Peter himself."

Candidate: "If I were Saint Peter, you wouldn't be in my district."

Shortly after his defeat for reelection, a politician was introduced as follows by a toastmaster: "The next speaker bears a slight resemblance to the earth. You know the earth is not a perfect spheroid because it is flattened at the poles. So was your next speaker."

Election Agent: "That was a good, long speech our candidate made on the farming question, wasn't it?"

Farmer: "It wasn't so bad; but a couple of nights of good rain would have done a sight more good."

Three men were arguing over which profession was the oldest.

Said the surgeon: "The Bible says Eve was made by carving a rib out of Adam. I guess that makes mine the oldest profession."

"Not at all," said the engineer. "In six days the earth was created out of chaos—and that was an engineer's job."

Said the politician: "Yes, but who created the chaos?"

Psychiatry

The neurotic builds castles in the sky. The psychotic lives in them. The psychiatrist collects the rent.

A modern mother, finding some difficulty in getting her young son to take a spoonful of castor oil, reminded him, "Now Wilbur, all you have to do is to keep saying to yourself, 'It tastes good! It tastes good!' and it won't be hard to take at all."

Suddenly Wilbur had an inspiration, "Mother," he cried, "I know a better thing to say. I'll say, 'I've already taken it! I've already taken it!' and then I won't have to take it at all."

Psychology tells us that it is bad to be an orphan, terrible to be an only child, damaging to be the youngest, crushing to be the middle, and taxing to be the oldest. There's no way out except to be born an adult.

A woman took her husband, wearing his Napoleon outfit, to a psychiatrist. "It's so embarrassing," explained the wife. "He tells everyone he's Julius Caesar."

A woman visited a psychiatrist and said, "You've got to help my husband. He has delusions and thinks he's an elevator."

"You send him in to see me," replied the psychiatrist, "and I'll try to straighten him out."

"Oh, I can't do that," answered the wife. "He's an express and doesn't stop at your floor."

A friendly psychiatrist saw a psychologist struggling down Connecticut Avenue in Washington, D.C., carrying a couch on his head. "Why the couch?" he asked.

"House calls," was the burdened reply.

The psychologists say you can cure insomnia with autosuggestion. You just lie there telling yourself, "I'm a night watchman — I'm a night watchman." The first thing you know, you'll be sound asleep."

Psychiatrist: "Congratulations, you're cured."
Patient: "Some cure! Before I came to you I was Napoleon. Now I'm just another nobody!"

A psychiatrist told a story about a patient he felt was making good progress in the cure of a split personality.

"I was optimistic," confessed the psychiatrist, "until this patient called and demanded to know why he'd received only one bill."

Patient: "I feel schizophrenic."
Psychologist: "Well, that makes four of us."

Letter to psychiatrist from patient: "Having a good time. Why?"

Sign on a psychiatrist's office: "Amnesia patients must pay in advance."

Psychiatrist: "Now tell me about this dream you had."
Lady Patient: "Well, I dreamed I was walking down the street with nothing on but a hat."
Psychiatrist: "And you were embarrassed?"
Lady Patient: "I certainly was. It was last year's hat."

Real Estate

"My new development," the real estate broker told a friend, "will have swimming pools and playgrounds for the children, tennis courts and softball diamonds for the grown-ups, not to mention the wonderfully paved roads and neon street lighting, a nearby shopping plaza, and excellent bus service."

"And what type of houses are you building?" asked the friend.

"Of course!" said the broker, "I knew I forgot something."

RESTRICTED BUILDING AREA: An area where no one is allowed to build a house that they can afford.

A suburban lady who was not only disagreeable but also a bit of a snob was chatting over the fence with a neighbor.

"We're going to be living in a better neighborhood soon," she said.

"So are we," replied the neighbor.

"Oh, are you moving too?" the snob wanted to know.

"No," said the neighbor, smiling sweetly. "We're staying right here."

Salesmen

A lady walked into an appliance store and asked to see some toasters. A high-pressure salesman decided instead to sell her an expensive freezer. "Madame," he pitched, "believe me when I tell you this freezer will pay for itself in no time at all."

"Fine," said the lady. "As soon as it does, send it over."

An exasperated salesman abandoned his car in a no-parking zone and left this note:

> I've circled this block 20 times. I have an appointment and must keep it or lose my job. "Forgive us our trespasses."

Upon returning, he found this note:

> I've circled this block 20 years. If I don't give you a ticket, I'll lose my job. "Lead us not into temptation."

"It's actually a fire sale," said the tired, worn-looking salesman. "If I don't make a sale, I'm fired."

An energetic vacuum cleaner salesman was giving his sales pitch to a backwoods farmer's wife. He threw a handful of dirt on her linoleum floor and announced, "If my vacuum cleaner won't pick that up, I'll eat it!"

"Get to work, young man," she said, "cause we ain't got no electricity."

A traveling salesman was driving by a backwoods farm house early one morning and saw an unusual sight. An elderly man was chopping wood dressed only in his long-handled underwear. When the salesman inquired as to why the old man was out chopping wood in such cold weather dressed so scantily, he was given the answer, "I been dressing by a warm fire for fifty years, and I'm not going to change now."

First Salesman: "My wife says if I don't give up golf she'll leave me."

Second Salesman: "Mercy, that's hard luck."

First Salesman: "Yes, I'm going to miss her."

Employee: "I've been with you twenty-five years, and I've never asked for a raise before."

Employer: "That's why you've been with me for twenty-five years."

Sayings

The latest thing in men's clothing today is women.

He who falls in love with himself is not apt to have much competition.

Be a patient pedestrian — avoid being a pedestrian patient.

The safest way to knock the chip off a fellow's shoulder is by patting him on the back.

Good luck will help you over a ditch — if you jump hard enough.

Years ago if people missed a stagecoach they were content to wait two or three days for the next one. Now they get exasperated if they miss one section of a revolving door.

You can't fool all the people all the time, but those highway interchange signs come pretty close.

Those who complain about the way the ball bounces are often the ones who dropped it.

Chewing gum proves that you can have motion without progress.

One trouble with today's individualists is that they are getting harder and harder to tell apart.

I'm neither for nor against apathy.

A person who can smile when things go wrong has probably just thought of someone he can blame.

Be friendly with the people you know. If it were not for them, you'd be a total stranger.

A chain of thought is no stronger than its weakest think.

He who parrots another's opinions instead of arriving at his own is not wise — he's just likewise.

What this country needs more than anything else is fewer people telling this country what it needs more than anything else.

A clever person puts his problems aside for a brainy day.

It usually takes more than three weeks to prepare a good impromptu speech.

Overeating reduces the life span.

The idea for daylight saving time came from an old Indian chief who cut off one end of his blanket and had it sewed on the other end to make the blanket longer.

The reason the dog is known as man's best friend is probably because he gives no advice, never tries to borrow money, and has no in-laws.

We'd have less trouble in this country today had the Indians enforced stricter immigration laws.

Where you go in the hereafter depends on what you go after here.

Speak well of your enemies. After all, you made them.

Home is where a fellow goes when he is tired of being nice to people.

Even if you are on the right track, you will get run over if you just sit there.

Most church members think an epistle is the wife of an apostle.

Some people can stay longer in an hour than others can in a week.

Keep smiling. It makes everyone wonder what you're up to.

You don't have to be listed in *Who's Who* to know what's what.

No generalization is wholly true, including this one.

Never miss an opportunity to make others happy, even if you have to let them alone to do it.

People green with envy are ripe for trouble.

The class yell of the school of experience is "Ouch!"

School

A mother was having a hard time getting her son to attend school one morning. "Nobody likes me at school," said the son. "The teachers don't and the kids don't. The superintendent wants to transfer me, the bus drivers hate me, the school board wants me to drop out, and the custodians have it in for me. I don't want to go."

"You've got to go," insisted the mother. "You're healthy. You've a lot to learn. You've got something to offer others. You're a leader. Besides, you're forty-nine years of age. You're the principal, and you've got to go to school!"

After several hours of trying to put a newly-bought gadget together according to the instruction sheet, the buyer, in desperation, took it down to the old gardener who was working in the yard. The old man looked at the gadget for a minute and then quickly assembled it. "It's amazing how you got that together without even looking at the instructions," the man said.

"Son," said the oldster. "I can't read. And if ye can't read, ye've got to think."

The teacher was explaining: "Quite a number of plants and flowers have the prefix 'dog.' There's the dog rose and the dog violet, for instance. Can any pupil name another?"

There was a silence, then a happy look appeared on the face of one of the youngsters.

"Please, teacher," he asked politely, "how about collie-flower?"

Teacher: "We get fur from the beaver, mink, and muskrat. Do we get fur from the skunk?"

Eric: "Yes, Ma'am, as fur as we can."

The safety sign read: "School—Go slow—Don't kill a child."

Beneath it was written in a childish scrawl: "Wait for a teacher."

For the third straight time, the little boy had brought home a terrible report card. After reading it with a shudder, the lad's father signed it with an *X.*

"Why did you do that?" the boy asked.

"I don't want the teacher to think that anyone with marks like that has a father who can read and write," the father replied.

After a particularly trying day, two teachers were discussing their hectic lives over coffee in the faculty lounge. Said one, "If there's anything to this business of reincarnation, I'd like to come back as a childhood disease."

A grade-school teacher asked her class to write a composition on "What Easter Means to Me." One student wrote: "Egg salad sandwiches for the next two weeks."

The assignment was given in the journalism class by the teacher: "Each member of the class is asked to write your most sensational three-word headline."

These two won honorable mention:

"President Declares War."

"McDonald's Closes Down."

However, the student who won first place used only two words: "Pope Elopes."

The school teacher got a note from Andy's mother that read, "My son, Andy, is a very sensitive boy. If you have to punish him, just slap the child in the next seat. That will frighten Andy."

A problem child was becoming too well acquainted with the principal's office. One day the principal remarked with annoyance, "This makes the fifth time I've punished you this week. What have you to say for yourself?"

"I'm glad it's Friday," was the quick reply.

Wife to husband who was reluctant to help their small son with his homework: "Help him now while you can. Next year he goes into the fourth grade."

Teacher: "What is the formula for water?"

Danny: "H,I,J,K,L,M,N,O."

Teacher: "That's not the formula I gave you."

Danny: "I thought it was. You said the formula was *H* to *O*."

"No wonder Monette gets straight *A*'s in French," lamented one teen to another. "Her parents were born in Paris and speak French at home."

"In that case I ought to get *A*'s in geometry," complained the other. "My parents are square and talk in circles."

The teacher had asked her pupils who the nine greatest Americans were. All pupils had turned in their papers except David.

"Can't you finish your list, David?" asked the teacher.

"I'm still undecided," he replied, "about the first baseman."

Prof: "That written essay you handed in was great. May I ask who wrote it for you?"

Coed: "I'm glad you liked it. May I ask who read it to you?"

A poor student was explaining his grades to his irate father. "You just can't beat the system, Dad. Last semester I decided to take basket-weaving. It's a snap course, and I figured I would sail through. Know what happened? Two Navajos enrolled, raised the class average, and I flunked."

One of the questions asked on a character test given at a junior high school was: "If you were in the rest room and saw a boy knock a hole in the plaster with a baseball bat, you would: (a) tell proper authorities; (b) laugh about it; (c) not want to be a tattletale; (d) not tell for fear of retaliation."

One girl did not check any of these answers but simply wrote, "Realizing I was in the wrong bathroom, I would get out of there in a hurry."

The first-grade class members were having a wonderful time playing with a stray cat. After a while one little lad asked the teacher if it were a boy or a girl cat. Not wishing to get into that particular subject, the teacher said that she didn't believe she could tell. "I know how we can find out," said the boy.

"All right," said the teacher, resigning herself to the inevitable. "How can we find out?"

"We can vote," said the child.

Before Thanksgiving a first-grade teacher asked her pupils to tell her what they had to be thankful for. "I am thankful," said one small boy, "that I am not a turkey."

To stimulate her young pupils, a first-grade teacher arranged to take her class on an "educational tour" of a farmyard. But one small boy saw right through her scheme. "Don't look, don't look!" he warned his buddy. "If we look, we'll have to tell about it tomorrow!"

A very small boy came home almost in tears from his first day at school. "I'm not going tomorrow," he spluttered.

"And why not, Son?" his mother asked.

"Well, I can't write and I can't read, and they won't let me talk, so what's the use?"

Johnny: "Say, Dad, do you know you're a lucky man?"
Father: "How is that, Son?"
Johnny: "You won't have to buy new books for me this year. I'm taking last year's work over again.

Sermons

Remark to pastor after the worship service: "Every sermon you preach is better than the next one."

A guest preacher stepped up to the podium and addressed his audience with these words: "As I understand it, my job is to preach, your job is to listen. If you finish before I do, please let me know."

A pastor, already having preached about an hour, noticed one of his members sleeping. Embarrassed, he motioned for an usher. The usher located the sleeping man and, taking a long stick, gently tapped him. The man snored on. The usher tapped him again, but a little firmer. The man continued to enjoy slumber.

By this time the usher's face was red with embarrassment, and it was then that he soundly whacked the gentleman's head. The man slumped from the pew and onto the floor. Thinking he had really injured the man, the usher knelt at his side only to hear him mutter, "Hit me again. I can still hear him."

Question: What two things are most helped by shortening?
Answer: Biscuits and sermons.

The minister's sermon concerned the relationship between fact and faith. "That you are sitting before me in this church," he said, "is fact. That I am standing, speaking from this pulpit, is fact. But it is only faith that makes me believe anyone is listening."

A minister gave an unusual sermon one day, using a peanut to make several important points about the wisdom of God in nature. One of the members greeted him at the door and said, "Very interesting, Reverend. Today we learned a lot from a nut."

A guide in London's Westminster Abbey advised an American tourist, "Many of the leading citizens of the Empire sleep all over this church."

"We have the same problem in America," said the tourist. "But we either improve the ventilation or get another preacher."

Smoking

A tobacco company heard that an old man living up in the hills had been smoking their particular brand all of his life and was now over a hundred years old.

The company wrote him a letter and invited him to come to New York, spend the night in a famous hotel, and appear on a nationwide television program at ten o'clock in the morning to give a testimonial for their tobacco.

The old man wrote a very short letter back and said, "I can't do it."

The tobacco company called. "We're calling you about our letter. We still want you to come to New York, spend the night, and appear on a television program at ten o'clock in the morning to give a testimony for our tobacco."

The old man answered, "I can't do it."

"You mean to say you don't want a free trip to New York?"

"Oh," the old man said, "that would be fine. However, I cannot appear on your television show at ten o'clock in the morning."

"Why?" asked the tobacco executive.

"Cause I don't stop coughing until noon every day."

He was a fanatic about smoking. Whenever he saw someone smoking a cigarette or cigar, he would pull it out of the person's mouth and step on it. He died of cancer of the foot.

"Wonder drugs won't help you," the doctor told his elderly patient. "What you need is complete rest and a change of living. Go to a quiet country place for a month. Go to bed early, eat lots of vegetables, drink plenty of good, rich milk, and smoke only one cigar a day."

A month later the man returned to the doctor's office. He looked like a new man.

"Yes, Doctor," the patient said, "your advice certainly did me a world of good. I went to bed early and did all the other things you told me. But that one cigar a day almost killed me at first. It's not easy to start smoking at my age!"

A prisoner, about to be executed, was blindfolded. The captain of the execution squad asked him if he would like a cigarette.

"No thanks," said the prisoner, "I'm trying to quit."

Pipe smokers are almost invariably solid, reliable citizens. They spend so much time cleaning, filling, and fooling with their pipes they don't have time to get into trouble.

"I want you to give up smoking," the psychiatrist told his patient.

"Will that help me?" the patient asked.

"No," answered the psychiatrist, "but it will help me; you've burned three holes in my couch."

Speaking

Some talkative people never discover why they were given two ears and only one tongue.

Those who boast about having an open mind often have an open mouth to match.

A Martian landed on earth right in front of a filling station. Facing one of the pumps he said, "Take me to your leader." He repeated the command five times. Finally he yelled at the pump in a loud voice. "You might hear me better," he shouted, "if you took your tail out of your ear."

SPEECH FORMULA: Be sincere, be succinct, be seated.

One important thing a speaker should remember: The mind can absorb only what the seat can endure.

"Blessed are those who have nothing to say and who cannot be persuaded to say it."

"Did you make the debating team?"
"N-n-no. They s-s-said I w-w-wasn't t-t-tall enough."

Leroy: "Why do you say Jerry Don is noted for his after-dinner speaking?"

Billy: "He always manages to be speaking on the telephone when the waiter brings the check for the meal."

An African chieftain flew to London for a visit and was met at the airport by newsmen. "Good morning, Chief," one said. "Did you have a comfortable flight?"

The chief made a series of raucous noises—"honk, oink, screech, whistle, z-z-z-"—then added in perfect English, "Yes, very pleasant, indeed."

"And how long do you plan to stay?" asked the reporter.

Prefacing his remarks with the same noises, the chief answered, "About three weeks, I think."

"Tell me, Chief," inquired the baffled reporter, "where did you learn to speak such flawless English?"

After the now standard "honk, oink, screech, whistle, and z-z-z," the chief said, "Short-wave radio."

A doctor addressing a gathering told reporters that as he was making the same speech the following week in a neighboring town, he did not wish to have anything published. The following day he was horrified to read in the local paper:

"Doctor Smith delivered an excellent lecture—he told some wonderful stories—unfortunately they cannot be published."

With the metric system of weights and measures in effect, we will be speaking in terms of meters, millimeters, grams, kilograms, liters, etc., instead of pounds and miles and pints. This will mean, of course, that many of our old sayings and proverbs will have to be brought up to date. Examples:

"Give a man 2.54 centimers and he'll take 1.609 kilometers."

"28.350 grams of prevention is worth 453.592 grams of cure."

"Peter Piper picked 8.810 liters of pickled peppers."

"A miss is as good as 1.609 kilometers."

"Spare the 5.0292 meters and spoil the child."

"A journey of 1,609 kilometers begins with a single step."

"Put your best 0.3048 meter forward."

Sports

Golfer: "I'd move heaven and earth to be able to break a hundred."

Caddy: "Try heaven. You've already moved most of the earth."

Golfer: "I'm anxious to make this shot. That's my mother-in-law up there on the club house porch."

Friend: "Don't be silly. You can't hit her from here. It's over three hundred yards."

A man who was a golfing bug married a woman who loved to attend auction sales. Both talked in their sleep. One night the husband yelled: "Fore!"

The wife promptly shouted, "Four twenty-five!"

A college senior pointed to a substitute going into a

football game and said to his date, "I expect that guy to be our best man next year."

"Oh, dear," she blushed. "This is so sudden."

"I'm sick and tired of being left alone every weekend," grumbled the golf widow. "If you think you're going to play today, you've got another think coming."

"Nonsense," replied the husband, reaching for the toast, "Golf is the fartherest thing from my mind. Now, would you please pass the putter?"

A businessman joined a swanky club although he knew nothing about the game of golf. His first time on the course, his caddy handed him a driver for the tee off but the man refused and demanded a putter. The caddy protested he'd never make the 425-foot-long hole, but the man insisted and, to his caddy's astonishment, slammed the ball 240 yards. For his second shot he refused the caddy's suggestion of a No. 2 iron and, amazingly, landed on the green with a No. 9 iron. Then to sink the putt, he asked for a driver. This time the caddy argued vehemently but the man threatened to fire him if he didn't shut up, and sure enough, he sank the ball in the hole.

"Now's your chance," he told the caddy. "What do I use to get it out?"

Ralph Nader had some golf clubs recalled. They weren't up to par.

Two wealthy oilmen decided to play golf for the first time. On the way to a country club they purchased all the necessary equipment—shoes, sport togs, clubs, and so forth—then checked in at the club. "I'm sorry," the starter told them, "but you can't play today."

"But why not?" they protested. "Look—we're all ready. New clubs, everything."

"Sorry," repeated the starter, "but you can't play today. There aren't any caddies."

The oilmen looked at each other, "So, who cares?" said one. "For one day we'll take a Buick."

A golfing parson, badly beaten by an elderly parishioner, returned to the clubhouse depressed.

"Cheer up," said his opponent. "Remember, you win eventually. You'll be burying me someday."

"Yes," said the parson. "But even then it'll be your hole."

In an amateur golf tournament, a player was carefully lining up his putt when a ball whizzed past his ear and landed on the green. After the foursome putted out, the golfer who had made the unnerving approach hurried up to his near victim. "Gosh, I'm sorry," he said. "I would have yelled, 'Fore!' but I didn't want to ruin your putt."

The college football coach called practice to a halt to "chew out" one of his big freshman tackles for making a stupid play. Head bowed, the big tackle stood in silence as the coach called him every kind of name, topping off the blast with, "What's your IQ anyway?"

Startled, the tackle looked up, thought for a moment, then answered, "20-20."

He was a baseball fanatic. Without hesitation he could rattle off batting averages, home runs, and runs-batted-in for every player. Praising him for his memory, a stranger asked, "Do you ever forget your wedding anniversary?"

"Never!" he answered. "I was married the day Bobby Thomson hit the home run that won the pennant for the Giants. I'll never forget that day."

A football coach was asked by a fellow coach how he picked a team from a bunch of raw recruits.

"I hate to give away my secrets," he replied, "but I'll tell you. I take them out into the woods. Then at a given signal, I start them running. Those that run around the trees are chosen as guards; those that run into the trees are chosen as tackles."

Wife: "Why don't you play golf with George anymore?"
Husband: "Would you play golf with a man who moves the ball and puts down the wrong score while you're not looking?"
Wife: "I certainly would not!"
Husband: "Well, neither will George."

A basketball coach who is also an ardent boxing fan often has to miss the fights shown on TV because of scheduled games. One night an important bout was coming up, and he asked his wife to watch for him and tell him the results. After the game he rushed home eagerly. "Who won?" he asked.

"Oh," said his wife, "nobody won. One of the men got hurt in the first round and they had to quit."

A worn-out advertising executive was aghast when his doctor told him that every day he should jog the eight blocks from his apartment to his office, rolling a child's hoop. It was excellent therapy, the doctor said. If he didn't do it, he was in serious danger of cracking up altogether.

Thoroughly frightened, the advertising man bought a hoop and began dutifully banging it to and from work, parking it during the day in a garage. At the end of a week he felt so much better that he actually looked forward to his heroic stint. But one evening when he went to the garage to pick up the hoop, it was gone.

"I don't know how it could have happened, Sir," the garage manager said, "But it's our responsibility, and we'll pay for it."

The advertising man turned white, then crimson. "Pay for it!" he stormed. "Of course you'll pay for it! But what good is that going to do me? How am I going to get home tonight?"

Sunday School

Asked by his mother what he'd learned in Sunday School, ten-year-old Bobby launched into an exciting tale: "Teacher told us about when God sent Moses behind the enemy lines to rescue the Israelites from the Egyptians. When they came to the Red Sea, Moses called for the engineers to build a pontoon bridge. And after they had all crossed, they looked back and saw the Egyptian tanks coming. Moses radioed headquarters on his walkie-talkie to send bombers to blow up the bridge, and saved the Israelites."

"Bobby!" said his mother. "Is that the way your teacher told you that story?"

"Well, not exactly," the boy admitted. "But if I told it her way, you'd never believe it."

A Sunday School teacher asked little Mike to name his favorite miracle. Mike replied, "I like the one where everybody loafs and fishes."

A Sunday School teacher asked a class of young boys to bring an object to Sunday School class next Sunday and quote a verse of Scripture that related to that object.

One enterprising young lad brought a candle and quoted, "Ye are the light of the world" (Matt. 5:14).

Another brought a shaker of salt and quoted the familiar verse, "Ye are the salt of the earth" (Matt. 5:13).

A third young man brought a small bantam egg and quoted the verse, "She hath done what she could" (Mark 14:8).

The Sunday School teacher had just finished a detailed account of Jonah and the whale. "And now, Willie, can you tell us what lesson the story teaches?" she asked.

"Yes'm," replied Willie, "it teaches that you can't keep a good man down."

A Sunday School teacher asked her class how Noah spent his time in the ark. The youngsters seemed baffled. "Do you suppose, with all that water around him, he did a lot of fishing?" she asked.

"Ha," one redhead piped up. "With only two worms?"

The Sunday School teacher had just concluded a review of the day's lesson. "And now, children," she inquired, "who can tell me what we must do before we can expect forgiveness of sin?"

There was a pause, but finally one little boy spoke up. "Well," he mused, "first we've got to sin."

Tact

A meek little man in a restaurant timidly touched the arm of a man putting on an overcoat. "Excuse me," he said, "but do you happen to be Mr. Smith of Newport?"

"No, I'm not!" the man answered impatiently.

"Oh—er—well," stammered the first man, "you see, I am, and that's his overcoat you're putting on."

A widow asked a young man to guess her age.

"I have several ideas," said the tactful young man with a smile. "The only trouble is that I hesitate whether to make you ten years younger on account of your looks or ten years older on account of your intelligence."

"How do you like my hat?" asked a young wife innocently, as she preened herself before the mirror.

"It looks silly," said her tactless husband. "Why don't you return it?"

"Oh, I can't return it," was the reply. "You see, it's my old one. But since you don't like this one, I will go buy another one."

TACT—The ability to make your guests feel at home when you wish they were.

Priest: "When are you going to break down and eat ham?"
Rabbi: "At your wedding."

Two rival opera singers were making conversation with each other backstage at the opera house.

"I insured my voice for a half a million dollars," bragged one.

"And what," countered the other, "have you done with the money?"

A woman was attending her first baseball game.

"Isn't that pitcher grand!" she yelled. "He hits their bats no matter how they hold them!"

Teenagers

Angry Father: "Young man, what do you mean by bringing my daughter home at 3 o'clock in the morning?"
Young Man: "Well, Sir, I have to be at school at eight."

Curt: "I'm looking for a beautiful girl."
Betty: "Here I am."
Curt: "Swell. You can help me look."

TEENAGE LOVE—A feeling you feel when you feel that what you feel is a feeling you never felt before.

Paul: "You told me it was love at first sight when you started going out with Jane, but I don't see you around together any more."

Pal: "I took another look."

"Well, I sure told off that football tackle who took my girl friend out. I told him exactly what I thought of him, and I called him every name in the dictionary and plenty that aren't in it. Boy, I had him burning up!"

"Did he try to hit you?"

"He didn't. And when he tried to answer me back, I just hung up the telephone receiver and walked away."

No wonder today's teenager gets mixed up—half the adults are telling him to "find himself" and the other half are telling him to "get lost."

Many a girl who thinks she was bitten by the love bug discovers it was only a louse.

A teacher telling his class of teenagers about the old West said that Billy the Kid had killed twenty-one men before he was twenty-one years old.

A girl who had been listening openmouthed asked, "What make of car did he drive?"

Why can't life's problems hit us when we're eighteen and know all the answers?

Randy: "I thought I told you not to tell Mom how late I came in last night."
Marie: "I didn't tell her—I just told her I was too busy setting the breakfast table to notice the time."

Father (to teenage daughter): "I want you home by 11 o'clock."
Daughter: "But, Daddy, I am no longer a child!" she replied.
Father: "I know. That's why I want you home by 11."

A generation crisis in reverse occurred when a teenager drove his car into the garage and ran over his father's bicycle.

"Yes," said one mother to the other, "I used to have an awful time getting my teenage son up out of bed in time for school, but I discovered a technique that works. I just open his bedroom door and drop the cat on his bed."

"Humph," said the other, "that would never wake up my boy."

"It certainly does mine," said the first. "He sleeps with the dog."

Linguists reckon there are between 3,000 to 4,000 languages spoken throughout the world, not including that spoken by teenagers.

The way to keep your teenage daughter out of hot water is to put dirty dishes in it.

"What is the thing I'm most anxious to get out of my new car?" grinned a businessman in answer to an advertising expert's question.

"That's easy! My seventeen-year-old son."

A father was telling a neighbor how he stopped his son from being late to high school. "I bought him a car," he said.

"How did that stop him from being late?" the neighbor asked.

"Why, he's got to get there early to find a parking place."

A teenage son approached his father for an increase in his allowance. After delivering a lecture on the virtues of economy, the father added plaintively, "Don't you realize, Son, that there are more important things than money?"

"Of course," the boy replied, "that's the trouble."

"What trouble?" the father asked.

"Those important things cost money to date."

A proud sixteen-year-old turned into the family driveway at the wheel of the family car. His father sat beside him. Several younger brothers converged on the scene.

"I passed my driving test," shouted the happy driver. "You guys can all move up one bike."

The young girl assured her parents that she and her boyfriend were only half serious about getting married — "I am — he's not," she explained.

The mother of one teenager caught on fast to jive talk. Her daughter asked, "Mama, may I hit the flick?"

"I'm afraid I don't understand you."

"Oh, Mother," said the youngster, "you mean you don't know? 'Hit the flick' is teen talk for 'Go to the movies.'"

"In that case, ask me again after you rub the tub, scour the shower, spread the bed, and swish the dish."

A woman, trying to persuade her daughter to wear her hair in a shorter style, lost the argument when her daughter offered this clincher: "But Mother, my date wears his hair longer than that!"

"Just a trim," the teenage boy told the barber. "You can even it up a little around the shoulders."

A young man proposing to young lady — "Darling, when we get married, there will be nothing but sunshine in our lives. The dark clouds will all roll away and leave blue skies."

The young lady's reply, "Just put the ring on my finger and forget about the weather report."

Ben: "Did you hear about the karate expert that joined the army?"

Bob: "No, what happened?"

Ben: "The first time he saluted he nearly killed himself."

Teenager: "Father, when I get through college, I've decided I'm going to settle down and raise chickens."

Father: "Son, take my advice. Forget about the chickens and raise owls. Their hours will suit you better."

Telephone

In the midst of a busy morning, the country agricultural agent got a call from a woman who said she was starting a chicken farm and wanted to know how long she should leave the rooster with the hens.

"Just a minute," said the agent, who was busy talking on another phone.

"Thank you very much," said the woman and hung up.

The bathtub was invented in 1850 and the telephone in 1875. Had you been living in 1850 you could have sat in the bathtub for twenty-five years without the phone ringing once.

The customer asked the waitress for her telephone number. She promptly gave it to him. When he called, a voice answered, "Pest Control Service."

Would Alexander Graham Bell have invented the telephone if he'd had teenagers in his home?

Having dialed a wrong long-distance number, a woman frantically demanded, "Is June there?"

A man's deep voice replied, "No, Madam, I don't know where you are, but it's still April here."

A man on a party line wanted to make a call but found the line was already in use. "I put on a pot of beans for dinner," he heard one woman tell another.

"My, my, really?" said the other, "So did I."

Twenty minutes later when the man tried again to make the call, the same two women were still talking.

"Say, Lady," he interrupted, "I smell your beans burning!"

There were two simultaneous exclamations, two receivers were slammed, and the line was clear.

Television

The young son of a well-known television star came home from school with his report card.

"Well, Son," said the father, "were you promoted?"

"Better than that, Dad," replied the youngster. "I was held over for another twenty-six weeks."

The movie on educational television was a touching story of the hardships of the average family during the

French Revolution. But one lady was unimpressed. "It doesn't make sense," she announced to her companion. "If they were so poor, how could they afford all that antique furniture?"

An argument in favor of TV from a twelve-year-old: "Before TV, nobody even knew what a headache looked like."

Television is often referred to as a "medium" because it rarely comes well-done.

Vacation

A motorist was driving through a remote section of the country. After stopping in a small village for something to eat, he noticed that his wristwatch had stopped. As he paused on the porch of the small cafe, he turned to a native lounging nearby and said: "I wonder if you could tell me what time it is?"

"It's twelve o'clock," drawled the man.

"Only twelve o'clock?" questioned the traveler. "I thought it was much more than that."

"It's never more than that around this part of the country," replied the native. "It goes up to twelve o'clock and then starts all over again."

A woman on a train, describing her holiday to a man in the next seat, mentioned that she had visited San Jose.

"You pronounce that wrong," said the man. "It's San Ho-Say. In California all the *J*'s are pronounced as *H*'s. When did you visit?"

The woman thought a moment, then answered, "In Hune and Huly."

A vacationing family loaded its pet squirrel, cage and all, into the front luggage compartment of their foreign, rear-engine car. At a remote gas station in the mountains, the husband told the station attendant to "fill'er up," and the family stepped out to look at the beautiful view.

When they returned, the husband asked how much he owed.

"Don't rightly know," the attendant said. "I gave your engine two bags of peanuts — but I'll be jiggered if I know how to check its oil."

Weddings

After many months of courtship, a girl dismissed her suitor with the statement that she could not think of marrying him until he had a few thousand dollars.

A few months later she met him and asked how much he had saved up.

"Thirty-five dollars," was the reply.

"Well," she said with a blush, "I guess that's close enough."

The pretty young girl had just broken off her engagement with the young doctor.

151

"Do you mean to tell me," exclaimed her girl friend, "that he actually asked you to return all his presents?"

"Not only that," she replied, "but he also sent me a bill for forty-four house calls."

Weddings have become so costly that it's now the father of the bride who breaks down and weeps.

Smith: "What made you decide to put off your wedding by two days?"

Jones: "Well, you see, I figured out that my silver anniversary would come on a Saturday, and I always play golf on Saturdays."

A minister was planning a wedding at the close of the Sunday morning service. After the benediction he had planned to call the couple down to be married for a brief ceremony before the congregation. For the life of him, he couldn't think of the names of those who were to be married.

"Will those wanting to get married please come to the front?" he requested.

Immediately, nine single ladies, three widows, four widowers, and six single men stepped to the front.

Miscellaneous

Two cowboys were talking. One said, "My name's Tex."

The second one asked, "You from Texas?"

Answered the first one, "Nope, from Louisiana, but what man wants to be called Louise?"

The immigration officer demanded, "Name?"

"Sneeze," replied the Chinese proudly.

The official looked hard at him.

"Is that your Chinese name?"

"No, 'Melican' name," said the Oriental, blandly.

"Then let's have your native name."

"Ah Choo."

A moviegoer standing in line for nearly an hour finally reached the box office. "That'll be $4," said the girl behind the glass.

Glancing at the sign "Popular Prices" over the box office, the customer grumbled, "You call $4 a popular price?"

"Well," said the girl sweetly, "we like it."

Usher: "May I help you, Sir?"
Man: "I lost a caramel."
Usher: "Oh, I thought it was important."
Man: "It is! My teeth are in it."

You can always tell an egotist, but unfortunately you can't tell him much.

When two egotists meet, it is a case of an *I* for an *I*.

A railroad clerk was being pestered with questions by a traveler while people in a long line waited impatiently. The clerk decided to teach the difficult man a lesson.

"Upper or lower berth?" he asked.

"What's the difference?"

"Well, the difference is ten dollars. The lower berth is higher than the upper one. The higher price is for the lower. If you want it lower you have to go higher. We sell the upper lower than the lower. Most people don't like the lower upper, although it's low on account of being higher. When you occupy an upper you have to go up to bed and get down to get up."

During the war in the Pacific, a young Yank pilot landed his airplane on an aircraft carrier, dashed up to the bridge, and, as he was pulling his life jacket off over his head, recounted his day's work.

"What a day I had, Skipper!" he exclaimed. "Sunk a Jap cruiser, shot down seven Jap planes, and left a Jap battleship listing!"

As he finished pulling his life jacket up over his eyes, he heard, "Velly good, Yank, but you make one velly bad mistake."

A fellow walked into a restaurant, saw no one in attendance, so he pounded and shouted, "Where is everybody? I want some food."

A horse walked out of the back room. The man stared at him. The horse said calmly, "All right, you're making such a fuss. What do you want? Order up."

The man continued to stare at him. The horse repeated, "All right now, let's have it. What's your order?"

Finally the man asked, "Did the cow sell this place?"

A young man became a Catholic priest. Now his mother introduces him as, "My son, the Father."

An elevator operator grew tired of people asking him for the time, so he hung a clock in the elevator. Now all day long, people ask him, "Is that clock right?"

Nervous man: "I've got butterflies in my stomach."
Doctor: "Here, take an aspirin."
Nervous man: "I just did. Now they're playing Ping-Pong with it."

For eight days and nights Mr. Jones had been unable to sleep. All kinds of medicine had no effect whatsoever. In desperation the Jones family summoned a renowned hypnotist. He fastened a beady eye on Mr. Jones and chanted, "You are asleep, Mr. Jones! The shadows are closing about you. Soft music is lulling your senses. You are asleep! You are asleep!"

The anxious family looked at the ailing man—and, sure enough, he was asleep. "You're a miracle worker," the grateful son told the hypnotist and paid him a substantial bonus. The hypnotist departed in triumph. As the outside door closed, Mr. Jones opened one eye. "Say," he demanded, "is that lunatic gone yet?"

To remain a woman's ideal, a man must die a bachelor.

"I could have married anybody I pleased."

"Then why are you single?"

"I never pleased anybody."

"Now, Maggie," the lady said, "remember that when the duchess arrives you must say, 'Your Grace.' "

The moment arrived. Maggie hurried to the door, opened it, and solemnly said, "May the Lord make us truly thankful for what we are about to receive."

A young couple acquired a parakeet whose only vocabulary was, "Let's neck!"

A preacher heard about it and suggested they cage their bird with his bird whose only words were, "Let's pray."

When the birds were put together the couple's bird, as usual, said, "Let's neck," whereupon the preacher's bird replied, "My prayers have been answered!"

A missionary unexpectedly met a lion in the jungle. Not seeing any way to escape, he fell to his knees in prayer. He was comforted by seeing the lion kneeling next to him.

"Dear Brother, how delightful to join you in prayer when only a moment ago I feared for my life," the missionary said.

"Don't interrupt," said the lion, "I'm just saying grace."

A little girl was upstairs ready to say her nighttime prayers when she appeared at the head of the stairs and said, "I am ready to pray — anybody want anything?"

Six prominent men were named as pallbearers in the will of a man who had died penniless, owing each of them considerable sums.

"They have been wonderful creditors," the will said, "and I would like to have them carry me to the end."

The lady from the East wanted to know why Westerners were supposed to die with their boots on.

"Well, Ma'am," drawled the cowboy, "if we die with our boots on, it won't hurt our toes when we kick the bucket."

"Wouldn't it be neat to know the time and place that you were to die?" asked a frivolous teenage girl.

"What good would that be?" asked her boyfriend.

"I wouldn't show up," she said.

Epitaph on a hypochondriac's grave, "I told you I was sick."

A youthful minister was conducting the funeral service of one of his deacons. In his concluding remarks he mentioned that the soul had departed from the body, and he illustrated it with dramatic gestures by pointing to the corpse and declaring, "Folks, what you see here is just the shell—the nut has departed!"

One teenage boy complained that his girl friend had so much dental bridgework that he had to pay a toll when he kissed her.

He had only twelve hairs on his head but he was proud of each one. Every morning he would arise, count the hairs, and go to work thankful that he had twelve hairs. Then he started noticing that his hairs were falling out. He purchased all sorts of tonics and did everything possible to save his hairs. The countdown was almost daily, 11-10-9-8-7-6-5-4-3-2-1.

One morning he looked in the mirror and saw there was not one hair on his head. He exclaimed, "Oh no! I'm bald."

Men wear their hair in three ways—parted, unparted, and departed.

A noted ophthalmologist was called on to examine a young singer who complained his eyesight was fading. After careful examination, the doctor presented a comprehensive analysis of the singer's situation, which he summed up in three words: "Get a haircut!"

"Do you think this hair restorer is any good?" a man asked.

"It's certainly done me a world of good," replied the other man.

"Give you new hair?"

"No, a new ranch. I invented that hair restorer."

After the barber had finished with his next to the last customer, he said to a teenager with long hair, "Your turn."

The teenager replied, "Oh, I'm not waiting for a haircut."

The barber then asked, "Well, why have you been sitting here half the afternoon?"

The teenager replied, "I'm hiding from my father. This is the last place in the world he'd think to look for me."

Barber: "Your hair is turning gray."

Customer: "I'm not surprised. Can't you work a little faster?"

Two convicts in prison: "You know, I feel that just our being here makes this world a better place in which to live."

Twenty prisoners escaped from a chain gang. They got past the guard by posing as a giant charm bracelet.

A nervous prisoner kept annoying his jailer. Finally the jailer lost his patience. "Look here, Pete, for the last time, I give you my solemn word I'll let you know when it's 1996."

"All right," said the warden, "what's your complaint?"

The architect prisoner, just caught in an escape attempt, said, "The prison walls are not built to scale."

Three prisoners in a Soviet jail were comparing notes. "I was jailed for getting to work late," the first said.

"My crime," said the second, "is that I got to work too early."

"And I'm here," moaned the third, "because I arrived at my job exactly on time. They accused me of owning an American watch."

The warden of a prison sent a note around to inmates asking for suggestions on the kind of party they'd recommend to celebrate his twenty-fifth anniversary. The prisoners all had the same idea — open house.

A lonely destroyer skipper ran his ship with both strength and compassion, but he kept almost entirely to himself. He had one ritual, however, which puzzled his fellow officers almost beyond endurance. Every morning before coming up to the bridge he would unlock a special drawer in his desk, take out a strongbox, unlock it, remove a small scrap of paper, read it carefully, return it to the strongbox, replace the box in the drawer, and lock the drawer.

One day, during a heavy air attack the skipper was killed. After the funeral, his executive officer led a mad dash to the captain's cabin, unlocked the special drawer, removed the strongbox, unlocked it, removed the mysterious scrap of paper, and examined it carefully while his companions waited breathlessly. On it was written, "Port is left; starboard is right."

"Here's a special message from the admiral, Captain," reported the sailor. "It's to you personally, Sir."

"Read it to me!" snapped the captain.

The sailor read, "Of all the blundering, stupid, idiotic morons, you take the cake!"

"Have that decoded at once!" ordered the captain.